A Year at Sea: Sailing Solo around the North Atlantic

Matt Hughes

Copyright © 2013 Matt Hughes

All rights reserved.

The moral right of the author has been asserted

ISBN: 10- 1492921904
ISBN-13: 978-1492921905

No part of this book may be reproduced or transmitted in any form or by any means without permission from the author, except by a reviewer who wishes to quote brief passages for a review in a magazine, newspaper or broadcast.

Picture to accompany this book are on A year at Sea Facebook page. There is also a website ayearatsea.co.uk

To the three women who made this happen: Julia, who challenged the strength of my intention; Nic, who suggested going now; and Sally, who made me write it properly.

CONTENTS

	Acknowledgments	i
1	Bristol Channel: Setting Off	1
2	The Lead Up	8
3	Brittany: a holiday	12
4	Spain; beyond a holiday	24
5	Atlantic Spain; stability	50
6	Leaving Europe; a new challenge	59
7	Island Life: the start	75
8	Island Life continued	91
9	The Crossing	111
10	Grenada to St Lucia	123
11	Stories	137
12	Martinique to Guadeloupe	145
13	Antigua	155
14	East Crossing	170
15	The Azores: the final crossroads	176
16	To Scilly: the last long passage	181
17	Home: completing the loop	186

ACKNOWLEDGMENTS

Disappearing out of your life for a year is easy in principle but the practicalities take up a lot of time and energy. I had fantastic help from friends and relatives who took on onerous jobs for the year. Gavin looked after my house, Julian looked after my car and Tony looked after my stuff. Gill and Kat kept my spirits afloat when I lost them. I was lucky getting started with the boat: Rob Bingham is a brilliant surveyor and I had Mark, Rob, Scottish Dave and Andy in the first, tricky passages and Ali to put right my ignorance on boat electrics and other things around ownership.

I don't think I stopped learning from those around me throughout the whole year. You'll know who you are; you're in here. There are also the inspired speakers at the Wilderness Lectures in Bristol and the enthusiasm of Avon Outdoor Activities Club. The 'can do' attitude was great help in the preparations.

Lastly the University of West of England for made it so simple to take a year off work. So, to all: thank you.

PROLOGUE

I have absolutely no idea what day it is. I have been at sea so long. When every day is the same as the one before, and the one before that; when anything more than tomorrow becomes too hard to imagine, or anything before yesterday is just a thought, counting them just seems meaningless. The wind is blowing, from behind, as it has done, forever. It rolls the large, gentle, waves slowly up behind me. The sun has come up, and it has gone down. Nothing else has changed. I am on my own, in my own world, thirty two feet by ten, surrounded by sea and sky, alone in the darkness. Maybe, the closest people to me are in the Space Lab up there somewhere.

I am lying propped up in the cockpit, lulled by the waves; each one regular, and yet unique. In the clear sky ahead I can see the memory of where the sun set some time ago. There are stars; so many of them, so clear, so many unknown constellations. On the right, low on the horizon, is the Pole Star. It is small, significant only as a marker, to keep it on the beam, to keep me travelling west. The Plough has not yet risen. There is another constellation that looks a bit like a question mark. It goes around the Pole Star like a twenty four hour clock hand, but backwards. If I applied myself I could work out the time. But as I do so I lose myself in other thoughts. Above on the left is Orion, imperious with his shining belt. Somewhere, low on the left, the Southern Cross will rise towards morning. The only colour in this enormous sky is the reflection from the mast light. At the top I can see a glimmer of red and green.

The wind is a warm blanket from behind. It is coming from the Sahara, a thousand miles behind me. My t-shirt is uneeded; clothes are a habit left over from my life, on land, a long time ago. Thoughts, my constant visitors, leaving little trace, travel with the wind. I am lost, wandering with them. I am at peace.

A Year at Sea

1 BRISTOL CHANNEL: SETTING OFF

I wake in slight panic. It is night and the red, port light of a ship is clear, bright. It cannot be far away. It is big, it must be close. I try to work out how it got there and what to do. It is not right and neither is the feeling. In this complete calm, and at this distance, I should be able to see other parts of the ship. Struggling with effort I work it out. I am waking. The red light is on my phone charger; an LED. I am at home, in bed, in Bristol. Tomorrow I will go to work, as I have been for months. But, in waking, the year comes back to me, in pieces, in vivid detail, sharper than any photograph, brightly lit against the darkness of my bedroom.

Well here I am, anchored in a little river up from Brest. It is windy and the air is wet so I can't go out and explore but it is nice to sit and rest for a while. It was strange to leave Bristol. During all those months and weeks and days of preparation it hadn't really sunk in that I was really going. The preparation for getting out of the Bristol Channel took up so much thinking space. Even though more than fifty people turned up to my good bye drinks, my mind was so much on preparation that I didn't really see a distraction beyond Lands End.

When I asked people about their travels it always started with luggage and from a bus or train station. Their ticket is the principal timing point. But I was starting from Bristol Docks, ten minutes walk from my house. My start was governed by a combination of availability of Mark, my brother, and Rob, a sailing friend, to help me, and with the tides in the Bristol Channel. This bit of water is one of the most complicated navigation areas in the world. There is very little room for error. I had no bags. I had transferred my things from the house to the boat when I moved aboard.

We had set of at about eight thirty ready to be in Junction Lock for nine o'clock. The Lockmaster opened the little swing bridge and we went into the basin. While we were waiting two friends arrived to say goodbye; and then Rachel, another friend, appeared with her new baby. As she pointed out, I had to see him now as he would be walking by the time I got back. We chatted with them while we waited for the big bridge to swing. It being the beginning of the harbour festival the lock was crowded with boats coming in to Bristol. I miscounted how many and got it wrong going in. As yet more boats flooded out I had to do a quick reverse. My yacht is renowned for being difficult to reverse. It goes its own way. By the time I got sorted the lock was empty but my way to it was now blocked by all these boats waiting for their turn to go through Junction Lock into the harbour. Was this an omen for the year I wondered.

By the time we were past the gates the Lockmaster had everything ready and we descended the few feet to the river level. As way of conversation he asked where we were going.

"The Caribbean" I smugly replied, still not really believing it.

"Enjoy your day out then" he quipped back. The few miles journey down the Avon is peaceful. There on the bank were Rob's parents taking photos of us leaving; and then on to the Avonmouth bridge where I got clearance from Bristol VTS (a sort of water traffic control) to proceed into the Severn and the Bristol Channel. There was obviously some communication in the background as we were hailed back by them on the radio some time later.

"We hear you're setting off for the Caribbean" they called. "Have a good journey and see you next year."

The tides in the Severn are very fast. There is absolutely no point in trying to buck them as they go faster than my boat. So the trick is to use them like a travelator; to get on when going our way and anchor or moor up on the other six hours before stepping on again. I had originally intended to stop in Cardiff or anchor in Barry to wait out the first foul tide. However, we still had two hours of tide left at that point so we headed on. We picked a spot to anchor on the north coast of Somerset outside Porlock Weir. It was calm at first but, when the tide rose a bit, it got very choppy. With Safe Arrival rolling as if on a fairground ride I was trying to cook supper, feeling sick and trying to remember that this was a dream come true; that I was going to have some great times. But at that moment all I could think was how I was going to stand another 364 days of this.

The trouble with anchoring in the Bristol Channel is that the tide rises by up to over ten metres. This is not a problem in itself but the strength of it means that you have to be very careful that the anchor has bitten. For that you have to lay out at least four times the depth in anchor chain. That means at least forty metres laid out. But that also means hauling in forty metres – all by hand - against a strong tide. It took ten minutes even with two of us. We were exhausted.

We set off for Lundy as soon as we could. Although this meant an overnight journey it was worth it to get out of there. So far what little wind there was had been on the nose. We may not have been fast, we were doing four knots through the water, but the tide was adding another five and it felt a lot more; enough to make it a cold night when on watch. The boat rocked around all over the place. We arrived in Lundy after twenty two hours of travelling, we hadn't yet got the sails out and were tired and no one felt good. What a start. Just to make us feel worse the Challenger Wales arrived a few minutes later. She is a sixty seven foot yacht capable of tackling any ocean in the world. She was clean and sleek, full of happy bunnies. After we'd walked around the island and had some food, Rob and I went over in the dinghy to say hello. Well, really we wanted to snoop. They showed us around this amazon of a boat. She had generators, sails the size of a house and a kitchen bigger than most houses. She is used for charity work to get people who wouldn't normally get a chance to experience the outside life. Humbled, Rob and I returned to my small, slightly shabby "Safe Arrival." But, "she is mine." I thought, "and I'm off in her."

On the way to Padstow the next day we did do a bit of sailing. We tried out Mildred, the windvane self-steering system. (George is the electrical, compass steering system) Basically, a paddle sits in the water behind the boat, connected to a wind vane. If the boat goes off course then the wind vane makes the paddle twist, this then swings one way or the other in the water and the force of deflected water turns the tiller by way of ropes and pulleys. It is lovely to see and feel the boat steer itself. A few hours later we navigated ourselves around the Doom bar and into the tiny Padstow harbour. This only opens at high tide. All the rest of the time there is a gate closed to stop the harbour water running out to sea. We were welcomed by a large crowd listening to a brass band playing, al fresco, all the old, and new, favourites. It was all very jolly. We rafted up, the fourth boat on the outside, and proceeded to leave dirty footmarks on everyone else's boats as we crossed them. Motoring again, the next day, we dropped Rob off in St Ives. Unfortunately, his life jacket inflated automatically on the way back. At least I had a spare gas cartridge.

More motoring; this time the fifteen miles or so around to Lands End. There are two ways of rounding this headland: outside Long Ships lighthouse, or on the inshore passage. I've done the inshore several times before and was all set up when the visibility dropped. It's a strange thing owning my own yacht. In a charter yacht I'd probably have gone on anyway as it was not unsafe; just a little unsettling. The rocks of Land's End on one side and the rocks of Longships on the other are not far apart; but with a year's adventure beyond, and a little doubt in my mind, I bottled it and went around the outside. A few minutes later the visibility cleared up and we watched a couple of other yachts going through.

At last we had some wind and some proper sailing. Still in sight of Land's End we set course for Brittany. Mildred was keeping us on track while we settled down for a thumping good sail. That was it. We ate and made tea and took two hour watches and just enjoyed the sail. It feels good when you can feel the boat react to the wind and virtually skip along. The occasional wave would break right beside us, slapping the hull or sending spray up over us. As it got dark we put in a reef and I went off watch.

I woke to find Mark confused and concerned. A large ship had done what looked like a handbrake turn about a mile away. Why a thing the size of Selfridges would just stop sideways in the Channel is beyond me. But there it was. And in front of us we could see all the ships making their way around the corner of Brittany. This is the main route for shipping; the equivalent of the M25. They come through the English Channel, around Brittany and head towards Europe, Africa, Asia or straight on to the Americas. We were now approaching the West going lane. During my watch we crossed it. I had the radio close at hand, a very bright white scare flare and my eyes on full alert. Although you can't see them in the dark you can tell a ship is big because it has two white lights facing forward-ish, the front one lower than the aft one. These, and a red or green light on the side, show which way it is going. As we crossed a mile in front of one the feeling of knowing several thousand tons, represented by two white and both red and green lights, is heading straight at you. I always have this urge to put the engine on and make a fast exit. The trouble is that they are doing six times faster than we could ever do so there is no point. It is such a relief when they, or their radar, has seen us and they alter course slightly. The red or the green light disappears and I know that the several thousand tons has recognised that steam gives way to sail. So

Bristol Channel: setting off

into the central reservation and relative safety ready to tackle the Eastbound carriageway.

We reached L'aber Wrac'h about ten o'clock in the morning. It's an unsettling approach. Find a bunch of rocks and head straight for them. Before you hit them find two red roofs; line them up and head in along that line. This gives you the safe route between all the rocks. When at the end turn right and head up river. Once berthed and registered that was it; we went straight up into the old town and had a snack with coffee and a vin rouge. We were abroad at last. It had taken us four days to get to Lands End and twenty four hours to get to France. It was easy to tell we were in France: a crocodile of school children trotted by; the sailing instructors all had long wavy hair; and the brie kept trying to climb out of the bag on the way back to the boat.

To get round the North West corner of France to Brest we had to go through the Channel du Four. This has many horror stories to go with it. We timed our departure the next morning to catch the right tide and set off. It is the channel between Ouessant (Ushant) and the mainland. It is sprinkled with rocks, the tide runs fast and there are several changes in direction. It shows how much I respect it by that I set up the GPS like a satnav. It's not like me at all to use the GPS. We got lunch ready before hand and prepared for the equivalent of a white water ride. What an anticlimax. In light winds, clear blue sky and smooth seas Mark slept through most of it.

In Brest we found that there was a big party on . The new marina sits under the castle walls. All the young people of the town were out enjoying themselves in front of big stage that had been set up in the harbour. While various groups played, the young people promenaded and we sat in a bar, drinking beer and watching them. It was pleasant to sit there, knowing we had got somewhere at last.

The next morning Mark left. I now had a few days on my

own. It felt strange to be on my own after so many days in such close proximity. I realise now that I was too concerned with what I had to do to recognise any feelings beyond feeling strange. That would come later. I had a sleep after breakfast, ready to plan for food and where to go. I had to leave the marina because I couldn't afford the fees on my own. This was my first solo sailing. I spent a long time getting the ropes ready. Then thought that I would need the anchor later; so I got that ready as well. And then realised that I might be on a mooring buoy so got all the stuff ready for that as well. After all that I couldn't be bothered to change into sailing gear. I just threw my jacket over my t-shirt and set off. It all went well. But once in the Rade de Brest the rain swept in, the wind got up and, in wet jeans, wondered why I was doing this. I headed up a river until it got shallow, pulled over and dropped the anchor. It's been too inclement to go exploring so I now have a clean cooker, a chicken casserole and I have hung a vegetable net in the galley.

2 THE LEAD UP

It had all started a few years before. As a kid I had read Swallows and Amazons and been hooked on the idea of sailing. By the time I was eleven I had read the entire sailing section of my local library and I was fluent in all manner of sailing theory. All I needed now was somewhere to sail and something to sail in. Living behind Paddington Station, in central London, this presented something of a problem. We were not well off and had no car. The only local place to sail was at the Serpentine in Hyde Park where they had a couple dinghies as well as the rowing boats. However, they were too expensive for me and the quality of the boats was low. I searched for all the places to sail in London. But the problem was still that I had no boat. I even tried to get the head of physical education, at my school, to put sailing on the curriculum. I even suggested the ways that he could do it; but he smiled and explained that it was too complicated.

In the summer holidays, staying with cousins in Cornwall, I would cycle miles down to Rock, across from Padstow, and watch all the dinghies in the estuary. I could tell you all the types and designs, even the dimensions. I tried to get a friend to buy a dinghy with his Xmas present money. I look back now and realise that I was obsessed by sailing; and yet I'd hardly stepped in to a boat.

When I was fifteen I made a friend at school who was a member of the Ranelagh Sailing Club at Putney, on the Thames. He and I saved up money from our summer holiday jobs and managed to buy a National 12. We raced it Ranelagh for a couple of years before he sold his half to me. On average I must have raced two or three times a week over the next four years. At first we were poor at it but over time we improved. At the same time I was invited to go sailing in yachts on the Norfolk

Broads. The Green Wyvern Yachting Club was group of like minded yacht owners who took school kids on sailing holidays. It was different from sailing dinghies; the snail idea of the home on water, the slow and gently pace. It was cheap and fun. I was in my element.

I was also invited to join a sailing club that had a houseboat on the Norfolk Broads. The membership was mainly older teenagers sailing a few dinghies and a clinker, half-decked boat on day trips from Thurne. We also arranged weeks for ten to thirteen year olds. In my second year with them I lived on the houseboat right through the longest and hottest summer of my youth. From June to September I sailed to Potter Heigham each day to work in the boat yards or, on Saturdays, to clean and prime the chemical toilets at charter changeover. I was lucky to be offered a place at university in Norwich and, although in lesser amounts, I continued to sail occasionally.

My time in Norwich opened up my life in different directions. I came from a musical and generally artistic family. I was the unusual one. Good at maths and physics I had never considered the arts much. I'd built go-karts; modified bicycles; and renovated motorbikes with friends. We had even built a kind of land yacht. At university I made friends from the arts faculties. They introduced me to the study of literature, some of the ideas of paintings and architecture. They took me to hear Ian McEwan read. Although I had always read a lot I could begin to understand why I loved books like Brideshead Revisited so much. I could start to see why my photographs were OK and my friend's were so much better. With my retentive memory I could make the connections between allusions.

I would stay up all night with my housemates discussing Hamlet. We would make plans to live in Paris and write about existence; we would live in Madrid and write about bullfights; we would hitch-hike across America. I would be Satre. I would be Hemmingway. I would be Kerouac. I wanted to be an author. Slowly, sailing took a back seat. I gave up my Maths and Physics degree. I couldn't transfer to another course at Norwich so I went back to college for a literature exam and accepted a place at Bristol Polytechnic to study humanities. Here I was introduced to philosophy, communication studies, sociological and political interpretations and joined a drama group. In the lull of finishing the degree I took a job in the local hospital. Within a year I started a nursing course. At the same time I began a relationship that developed into a marriage and a family.

When I moved to Bristol I assumed that, as a maritime port with a long history of seafaring, I would find sailing opportunities easily. With the attitude that I hadn't sailed for a while but would again soon, it never occurred to me that I hadn't sailed for some years. While I lived a good life and enjoyed myself, I look back and realise that there was always a part of me that yearned for the water again. Every now and then it would rise, open up one eye and scan the horizon. I would meet someone who sailed, I would look down on a yacht in the harbour. It was deep down, a longing. It was twenty four years later that a friend invited me on a sailing holiday in Turkey. I jumped at the chance. Within minutes of being aboard I found that I had a vocabulary I'd completely forgotten. Kicking Strap, Topping Lift, Gybe; all these words just poured out. The skipper was intrigued as I went from rope to rope, adjusting and trimming the sails, my racing instincts released. Within weeks I'd done my Day Skipper course and within a couple of years had skippered trips to Scilly and Ireland on charter yachts. Over the next years I organised bare boat charters with friends all over the UK and several Mediterranean countries. I also achieved my Yacht Master Offshore qualification.

A friend lent me Robin Knox-Johnston's book. I was given Elen McArthur's book and I read Pete Goss as well. But, great reads though they were, all of these were great tales of courage and battles in the Southern Ocean. I was more interested in the softer, cruising world. I wanted to see places and meet other people and swim in warm waters. A circumnavigation interested me but it was too long a journey and too expensive. It would have to wait.

And then, one day, in a second hand bookshop, I came across a book "The Breath of Angels", completely in the wrong section, by a man, John Beattie, who had set off to sail around the world. He made loads of mistakes, ran out of money and by the time he had got to Tenerife had decided to do a North Atlantic Circuit instead. I'd never thought about this. It was a long time before I realised that this was the trade route for slaves and sugar that I had learnt about at school. I could do this; a year at sea. Within a few days I also discovered that I could retire in a few years so the time and money would be there. I began to think about it more and more over the next two years. Then, in the autumn, a friend asked why I wanted to retire for just a year's journey. I loved my job; it would be difficult to find anything better to do when I came back. Why not take a year off work? Within weeks my manager had agreed to it and Safe Arrival came on the market. She was set up for short-handed ocean sailing. The bank agreed a loan and by the new year I was set for departing in August. All I had to do was to get the boat around to Bristol and prepare her for the journey. In the space of two months I had gone from the idea, to having the time off, a yacht to do it in and the money to go. Now all I had to do was to plan the year away.

3 BRITTANY: A HOLIDAY

I am looking out for Chris. He flew into Brest yesterday but the busses didn't run late enough for him to get to La Turballe, on the east end of South Brittany, last night. He is arriving sometime today. Thinking of him arriving in Brest reminds me of meeting Simon and Barbara there. Simon and I had sailed a bit together on several occasions but we had met white water paddling. He was a very good paddler. He is one of those people who listens with an intent look while he takes it in. He gives the impression that what you are saying must be the most important thing in the world.

In the few days before they arrived I'd been resting up in the river above Brest. I'd had no idea how tired I was. This was the first time in months that I had nothing particular to do. After all that preparation, all those tasks to do on the boat, all that stuff getting the house ready to rent, all the thought about what I would need on the journey, all that navigation in the Bristol and English Channel; it was all over. I woke up at anchor in a pleasant river a few miles up from Brest. It was eight o'clock. My phone had just received a text. I went back to sleep. At ten thirty I awoke again; but then I woke again at twelve thirty.

I had a breakfast of brie and baguette and got the dinghy out. The book said there was a pretty town about four miles up river so I went to see it. I filled the outboard tank and set off in the dinghy to Landerneau. It was quite pretty but I didn't have too good an introduction. I had just secured the dinghy to a slipway when a man, fishing nearby, showed surprise that I was leaving it there.

"Manouche" he exclaimed. Once I remembered that the work meant gypsies I thought of Jonny Deppe arriving with an atrocious accent in the film Chocolat; but then reality caught up with me and I realised that I would be unlikely to see my dinghy again if I left it there. So I motored the last bit into town to moor under what seems to be the end of the river. A row of houses blocked me from going any further. This is one of those bridges that is completely built upon. And the buildings are all hundreds of years old. Really, the water flows through channels under them, but it is still a bridge.

I wandered around for a while and then sat in a cafe watching lotto fever. In the half hour I was there the waitress, who also sold cigarettes and lotto tickets had no more than a couple of minutes away from the counter as one after another they all piled in a bought their tickets – and cigarettes. After that I wandered around a little more, bought some food and wandered back to the dinghy. Innocently I checked the tank; it was nearly empty. I wasn't particularly worried. I just bent to the task of rowing back, quietly, often just gliding with the tide. It was a very peaceful four miles to be with just the birds and the banks and the water.

These days were full of new solo experiences. I set to weigh anchor with the windlass. This involves pushing and pulling a lever backwards and forwards; with each swing the anchor chain comes in by about ten centimetres. It is hard work. After about a 100 swings I tried pulling the chain in by hand. This was so much easier. Maybe the windlass needs some maintenance or else it is just difficult to use. Once I got the anchor off the bottom the boat started drifting down river. I then had to run backwards and forward to the helm to steer the boat while getting up the last bit of chain and the anchor into its home position.

The sails were up and we were away; except that I had to tack down the river and into the Rade de Brest. This is a narrow channel at that point so I had to keep watching the depth and tacking. Steering, winding in jib sheets, looking out for other boats; all in all it was a tiring experience. And then there appeared to be a race about to start. Tens and tens of brightly coloured yachts started appearing from a marina nearby. They were all decked out in sponsor's logos and obviously had the latest sail technology. It dawned on me that they were solo too. And here I was in the middle of them; a tatty old, but loved, Rival in the middle of all these graceful creatures.

They were going to race where I had intended to moor for the night. So, having miscalculated food provisions I decided to go back to Brest marina and wait for Simon and Barbara there. I put George, the auto pilot on but he just whined, whirred and gave up the ghost. That meant another new experience: getting the sails down while the boat tries to turn downwind and run away. I had to keep running back and forth again to the tiller to put her back on track.

Coming alongside the pontoons solo was, again, a new experience. I got everything ready for both sides and then went into the marina. Port side to; good; the easier side. I set up, came alongside, stopped the boat, jumped off and tied up the midships line; then a quick jump aboard again, motor in slow forward to hold her against the line and jump ashore again to tie up all the other lines. Perfect. Well not perfect but impressive. I was impressed. Well, I was relieved. I looked around and realised that there was no one was about to be impressed. To do all that and not have an audience.

Just then the marinera came alongside and told me that I had to move. There was a classic yacht party on here for the week and I would have to go to a finger pontoon deep in the heart of this enormous marina. So off with all the lines, off again and try again. This time I didn't do nearly so well. I nearly crashed the pontoon and there was no cleat to attach the midships line. Luckily there were two people to help; a mixed blessing as they were also my audience. They were very nice about it. In my stuttering French we talked about where we were going and that we would see each other later probably in another port. At that they checked their extra fenders. And then it poured with rain for the rest of the day.

Simon and Barbara arrived on a day with an anti-food motif. Having woken up reasonably early to get the boat ready for them I got lost in the internet. Having wifi again was a luxury, and I had shore power to run the lap top, so I indulged. The problem was that I forgot to have any lunch before going off to meet them. At the bus station they were just about to order a croc-monsieur. I stopped them to suggest lunch in a nicer looking restaurant down on the docks. But, having walked back to put all their stuff on the boat, we found that it had stopped serving. So had all the other restaurants. We had to wander back to the boat for a makeshift lunch from what I had left. After a catch up chat we realised that it was now too late for the supermarket. We went to eat in a restaurant that night.

Perhaps this food problem was some form of retribution. When in a foreign country a yacht must fly a courtesy flag of that nation. I had been flying the Dutch flag by mistake since arriving in France. No one had said anything. I wondered if they'd even noticed. They are the same colours but the stripes are horizontal on the Dutch flag. Two years ago I was in a pub in Bristol when a friend had called me across. He introduced me to someone who was off to sail a North Atlantic circuit in a few days time. This year, I had bought some yachting stuff off the internet forums. On sending my address for delivery one vendor had said that, as he lived around the corner, could he drop the pilot books off by hand. Blow, me it was the same man; he'd taken two years circuit. He also had some courtesy flags of several nations that I could use so I bought them off him too. It wasn't until I'd been in France several days that I noticed that we'd mistaken the Dutch one for the Tricolour. Since I bought the correct one in Audierne we've eaten well ever since.

I took the shore power off. There are a few things to do when preparing the boat to sail. From a marina berth you have to disengage all the umbilical appendages that come with the berth: topping up with water from your hose, getting the lines ready for departure and disconnecting the shore power. Theoretically, the regulations say that shore power leads should be plugged into the external side of the boat and pass through a flux capacitor, the sonic boom thrusters and some dilithium crystals before being used inside the boat. You can, at great expense, buy leads and sockets from chandleries to connect to these artifacts. Or you can go to a DIY store, buy an extension lead cheaply and not connect it to the boat at all. Mine was connected to an extension plug socket. It's a bit like running an extension lead from next door. All I used it for was the laptop and charging the batteries.

We were going for a shake down sail to Cameret, a small resort a few miles away. But as we were outside Camaret within an hour or so we decided to extend the day to Audierne. This involves going through the Raz de Sein, a small passage between a headland and the Isle de Sein a mile or so off. For some reason the tide swirls around this point and creates massive waves in any sort of blow. So long as the wind is light and in the same direction as the tide sailing it not too bad. But still, I have heard accounts of a standing wave two metres high, that can knock everything off your deck; something to be avoided. We reached it at slack water, the ideal time, and, although, superficially, it looked peaceful, we could still see the water swirling around, like octopus tentacles, in big eddies and occasional boiling crowns. I would love to see it in its fury - but from a safe vantage point.

Audierne is a small town up a silting river with a narrow, dredged channel. Carefully, nearing dusk, we nosed our way up to the marina. It was beautiful. The mixture of town, river and marina is enchantingly ramshackle. The boulangeries, the charcuteries, the cafes and tabacs line the old, stone quay front while half the boats are aground on the muddy shores, or tied up against the quay walls. It was just like their attitude to parking cars: "It is a space; we will park." This is real France. We were lucky; while trying to work out which bank of four-deep yachts we should raft up against I spotted an empty finger pontoon. Being small does have some advantages. We could get in there while the others couldn't. No grubbing over everyone else's boats for us. After a meal of stir-fried chicken aboard we strolled around the market in the town square. The old town is traffic free. The roads are two metres wide and wind up through the houses up to a couple of churches. In the odd space between two houses a boulangerie will tuck in, whiling away the day with customers.

Audierne certainly enchanted us. Spellbound, we forgot to check the tide times. We had to spend another night there or face a tricky night sail around lots of rocks and shallow water. We stayed and, in the sunshine, we sat on deck to watch the world. We ate lunch leisurely and wandered along for ice creams as pudding. We ate them sitting on the quay with our legs dangling over the rapidly rising waters while we watched the latest arrivals pick where to raft up. And in the early evening we were lulled to sleep by the quiet lapping of the river water on the hull.

Pointe de Penmarc'h is regarded as a border between north and south Brittany. We rounded it on the way to Concarneau with a light wind behind us. As such the architecture and feel does change a lot. In Concarneau the marina sits amongst the old docks just down from the fishing jetties. The fishing boats steam past at some two or three times the speed limit so we bounced around a bit in their wash. Also, the mooring lines rub on the toe rail and create an oompah sound inside the cabin. So I went to sleep dreaming of brass bands. It was not surprising really; on the dockside they had another festival playing with a brass pop band on. It sounded like a cross between Madness, the Keystone Cops and some snake charmers. But it did go on.

Brittany: a holiday

From Concarneau we decided to take a night sail to Belle isle. That meant that we could spend a day looking around. It is quite a tourist town because of the castle. I heard English voices here and there; it seemed like a long while since I could easily understand the background conversations. It took me back to my one and only reading of Ulysses when I was a student and aspiring to be an intellectual writer. The two stars, Leopold Bloom and his friend are walking back late at night when they hear some Italians talking. One remarks that Italian is a romantic language to which the other explains that they are having an argument about bus fares or something of that nature. While I hear French conversations at a speed too fast for me to understand I can still imagine that the dad is explaining to his kids that being is the essence to existence, or that boredom is an intellectual exercise. While I know that they are discussing which ice cream to buy I still liked to remember my university days and romantic notions of the entire French nation as existentialists.

Before we could be tourists I had some more mundane chores. I had need of a laundry. Choosing which clothes to take on the journey, before I left England, had taken some time. In the end it was easy. I think that was because, by that time, and with so many decisions, time was running out and I didn't care anymore. It was decision overload. It is quite strange to think of how many clothes I acquired over the years and how, now, I have had to hone these down to a bagful. They sit in little pockets around my cabin and I take one out each day. It's almost a random, lucky dip. After fourteen days I was low on clean clothes. I needed a laundry. So, in Concarneau, I went seeking one with my blue IKEA bag.

I hadn't been in laundromats since I was a student. All the instructions were in French (until after I had translated them when I noticed the English version.) Different programmes for different clothes? Pah! They all go in together; t-shirts, underwear, fleeces and bedding. By the time I get back I expect them all to be wearing the same greeny-beige no matter what I've got on. It seemed strange that on a Sunday morning there were so many different types in there. I saw the jeunes, possibly students, quietly folding all their stuff up once it was dry. The grumpy old guy huffed and puffed his clothes into the machines. The sporty guy had everything arranged in boxes. He had all his clothes, sorted, washed in turn and he placed the boxes back in order. On the other side there was the family with the wife who called "Cherie, Cherie" across to her husband. He ignored her. She burst into laughter because I, having recognised the word, looked up and caught her eye. "Quel Cherie?" she then exclaimed.

The castle turned out to be a little bit of an anti-climax. It is a very interesting entity in that it has an entire village in it. You can get the sense of what it was like to live in the protective shadow of a medieval castle. However, the streets are one long procession of ice-cream parlours, restaurants and the odd up-market gift shop. The first we duly visited and the latter was of interest to Barbara. She was Hungarian by birth; her parents had moved to Sweden when she was young and then later to the UK. She was in the retail trade; gift shops. I was impressed by her attitude. To go on holiday on a yacht when she had never sailed before and with someone that she had not met takes a bit of bottle. Our conversations led to the retail business and future plans. We sat on the ramparts, looking over the marina and Safe Arrival, discussing plans. It was mainly their plans as my plans really don't go much further than returning to the UK. That was as much as I could store in my plan compartment at that moment.

We left the harbour that evening just before the evening arrivals piled in. The wind was in our favour. We rounded all the obstructions (a euphemism for rocks and wrecks) and set course for Belle Isle. When planning passages it is normal to expect a yacht to travel at about five knots. That's about ten kph. However, Safe Arrival is an old yacht. Although she travels quite well downwind, she is slow to windward so I tend to work on an average of four knots. With a fair wind we were travelling well; which meant that we would get there before daybreak. If going into a harbour or the suchlike with lights this is no problem. However, we were picking up an unlit mooring in the middle of lots of yachts. The idea of picking our way through a swinging bunch of expensive plastic, in an unknown place, in the dark was not conducive to sleep. So we were glad when the wind died a bit; but we were not so glad when it gave up the ghost. That meant we had to turn the engine on. That is not conducive to sleep either. I was on off-watch for the two hours we had the engine on. I find it difficult to sleep with the drone it produces. I can hear every change its sound, wondering what it might mean. As I came up for my watch the wind picked up again and off we sailed, turning the engine off.

Sailing in the dark can be disorientating. As I watched a light house move past I could see little areas of darkness around it, sticking out towards the way we were going. In the Solent, if you see an area of darkness, a black hole where the stars disappear, then you look for the single red or green navigation light in the middle of it. You know it is a big ship the size of Selfridges approaching. These black holes were on the horizon, much smaller and seemed to be blocking out the street lighting on the land miles away. What could they be? If they were fishing boats then they would have lights. "Rocks" exploded in my brain. As carefully as I could I resisted the urge to turn tail. I carefully went below to look at (examine very carefully) the chart. No rocks. Up on deck again I re-examine the holes. After several repeats of this performance it dawns on me what they are: they are the areas of the coast that have no street lighting or housing. The lighting is not continuous along the coast; silly me. But I still keep an eye on them just in case.

Sauzon, on Belle Isle, was a bit like Kinsale in Ireland. It is a tasteful holiday resort full of bistros and restaurants. I'm beginning to wonder if French living units are provided with kitchens; they all seem to eat out all the time. Well, there were beaucoup de restaurants and they were full every night. We had a snooze in the morning before exploring. I'm beginning to realise that, by walking through new territory, conversations are stimulated about the past and future. Again, we chatted about plans while overlooking a beautifully regimented pattern of small boats set out in the drying river and inner harbour. But the smells of cooking food made us hungry and we went back to the boat for our own culinary exercises; salade al le roman, plus anything else we felt like throwing in. During the afternoon several other yachts arrived; they all waited for high tide so they could go into the harbour. They then all went ashore for a meal in a restaurant before departing the isle. It was obviously a place to eat out; a sort of nautical drive in.

The wind was disappointing for Simon and Barbara's last full day. After mooching along for an hour I stuck the motor on because, at that speed, we would not have got there until the next morning. But hey, they got their last sail in: as the wind picked up a bit we got out the cruising chute. Having played with it before we thought it should be easy. But somehow we had managed to twist it inside its snuffer. So we took it down below and packed it like a spinnaker. After that we put on half a knot. As the wind picked up further we started to semi-surf the waves. Safe Arrival was going faster than I had ever been in her. It wasn't long before we had to take the cruising chute down again or else she might have ripped open.

The almanac describes La Turballe visitor's pontoon as a place where yachts are boxed in. It couldn't be more apt. All the yachts are rafted up together in a three-sided pontoon with a small island pontoon in the middle. Each yacht that arrives chooses an optimum raft in a direction to suit them. As it fills up it is possible to walk from one pontoon to another across them. Mooring involves plenty of anxiety as all the previously moored yachts watch the next ones coming in. Deep down there is the horror that they may rev the engine in panic and an anchor may force its way through the side your boat. There is an advantage to being in a tatty old boat; no-one wants to get too near in case we pass on our tattiness. Also, we have Mildred, with lots of steel work, on the back and the anchor, ready to scratch, sticking out of the front. We had no one moored alongside us that night.

This was their last night. In the morning they left early. I was sad to see them go; it had been fun with Simon's constant desire to improve the boat efficiency – whether this was organising lines and plate fixings or trimming the sails – and Barbara's different perspectives on life from her background of Hungary and Sweden and retail. I was on my own again in my little floating house. In another way this was luxury. I could go back to sleep in my own bed for the first time in a week. I slept until ten o'clock when I realised that the majority of the marina was about to leave. It was like a merry-go-round with big bits of white plastic boat, lots of laughing and shouting, lots of observers and the occasional splash.

During the day it turned wet and windy. It wasn't so much rain as wet air; a warm front where you get soaked before you realise that you are wet. It feels like a spray from the shower and then it floods down your neck. In this I was trying to find Chris. I began to doubt my French as I tried to ask where the bus from La Baule would stop. I tried in the marina office where they understood my French easily but they were puzzled. They pointed to a spot on the map. I walked there but could not find anything resembling a bus station. Then I asked a little old lady in a doorway. She giggled as she shrugged her shoulders and told me that she only spoke French. So I reduced it to a very basic question. She shrugged again and told me something about the president. Maybe she wasn't altogether there; it did look very much like sheltered accommodation. So I asked in the charcuterie. They all gathered together and suggested ideas far too fast for me to gather more than a general idea of what they were saying. After a while they suggested that I tried the tourist information. There they told me that, peut etre, it might stop by the marina. But the time went by and it didn't. Back at the boat I got a text a while later from Chris to say that he was here. Tourist info had been right but the bus was late. It turns out that this is a little minibus and not a standard route, almost a taxi service; that's why no one knew what I was talking about.

I'd forgotten that he doesn't eat meat. But he does eat fish; neither Barbara nor Simon liked fish. We ate sardines that night. That was good; but I ate no meat for the next few days.

4 SPAIN: BEYOND A HOLIDAY

I have been doing lots of thinking about this journey in the last two or three weeks. Across Biscay we had faced up to the indifference of fate and what small control of our lives we have when at sea. After this came my emotions; the journey has varied from being sad and lonely to hilarious and great fun. In the middle of this I began to realise that I am a very social creature. Also, looking back, I have had good conversations with fellow crew but on my own a lot of things are jogging memories; living in the past. I started to question if this is what I wanted. John Beattie said, when he set off, that he could lose his life, his boat and his partner. I would add to this that I could lose my sanity. I need other people to bounce my crazy ideas off; people who can put some sort of rational framework on them. When I first had the ideas for teaching an online module years ago I needed my friends and colleagues to keep questioning me. Without that the ideas would have been so off the wall that it would probably have collapsed in the first run. As it was they added their bits and managed mine until we had a very good product.

Now, I had already lost my girlfriend. I had left La Coruna with dread. My head was spinning with nearly two weeks of my own ideas whizzing around. I wasn't living my dream. I was beginning to dread it. This wasn't how it was supposed to be. What could I do?

Chris and I had left La Turballe in sunshine and with a good Northerly wind blowing. I had been checking the forecasts regularly and it looked like light northerly winds for a few days. After a quick baguette run we set off. Someone had asked me whether it had sunk in yet that I was on a trip rather than a holiday. I wasn't sure. So far I had been on familiar waters until south of Brest. And then I had still been sailing in France and with someone I had sailed with before. Now I was into different territory. Firstly, I had not sailed a three day passage before. Secondly, Simon had been keen to keep sailing so the only time I had rested anywhere was in Brest. Now I was off to Spain, a place I'd not sailed before. It still felt like a sailing holiday. I wonder if that is how it goes: it only becomes a trip once it has passed. A bit like adventures only happen in the past; while you are there it is usually about survival.

I had plenty of time to think about this. The wind died away during the day and we flapped and flopped around in the swell. Every now and then, sporadically, repeatedly, a puff of wind would raise hope until, shortly, it would die again. For hours and hours this went on. Through the evening and into the night we swapped watches, two hours on, two hours off, and still nothing changed. We moved too few miles in too many hours. It was so frustrating. This was not Biscay. Biscay is about storms and finding weather windows to cross between them; not about glassy sea, slaps of swell on the hull and sunshine. In every direction we could see the water, not a ripple, lapping to the horizon; the haze of hot air blurring the gap between sea and sky into a blue grey smudge. The moon came up and changed the colour, but not the view.

An adjustment process seemed to be affecting both of us. There is a kind of navigation madness that sets in at sea. We looked at how far we had come and worked out when we would get there at this rate. We looked at how fast we were going and plotted the time again. We listened to the forecast again and tried to make it say what we wanted. In the back of our minds was the thought that Chris had a plane to catch on Sunday. Would we make it? We thought so. In one of the books I had read during planning it said to never plan a passage to a plane timetable. That way the relation is compromised. I took this in but thought that six days for a three day passage would be enough with time to spare. But it had taken Chris a day to get to me from Brest so he had lost one day already. A further adjustment was to the nights. Into the second night we knew that this was not to be the last. Somehow this made it harder to get up for my watch. I just wanted to sleep. On the third day out I noticed a subtle change. I started to do some maintenance while at sea. It was not the same as sorting things out when in harbour. There is only so much time you can make do at sea; after that we had to switch in to living maintenance rather than putting it off. It's a bit like you can be on holiday for three weeks but any longer and you revert to doing the things you need to do at home. It seems like two days is my limit. The batteries got low that night so we motored for a while to both charge them and see if we were in a wind hole. By that time we were serious about Chris missing his plane. We discussed contingency plans.

In the evening, just before twighlight, I was staring out over the swell when a school of porpoises appeared a little way off. There were about fifty of them on a parallel path to us. It was like a school, or multi-family, day out. There were some more staid ones at the front and back but the middle ones were out to have fun. One would leap out of the water by a good two feet. A few seconds later another would out do him. And another would jump higher still. The next one would add a twist to the leap and the next a twist and splash. The next few would see who could create the bigger splash. One of them swam on the surface, splashing for a good two minutes. The others joined in. And then several of them leaped in time to create a big splash, an ambush, next to an adult as he surfaced. For about half an hour this 200 metre natural circus stayed beside us. It cheered me up and made the day somehow more worthwhile.

It was warmer that night. We left the foulies off. The moon shone over the lolling sea again. Slowly a breeze built up enough for us to make slow but steady progress. Hurrah, we're off again. By morning we felt we had made something up on the journey. After a while the wind turned to the north east Force 4. Yes! We got the kite out for several hours and made the best progress yet. The wind got stronger and so we took it down again but still with a good speed. Like this we may get there by the next morning. This was navigator madness again; it died away and once again we slapped around. We tried to fly the kite again but it got twisted and ripped. What disappointment : Chris was going to miss his flight and I had lost my spinnaker. I slept for a while and then examined it; there was a two foot rip in one panel so probably not too bad. And anyway, we were close enough to motor in. It would be a twelve hour motor but we had to get Chris in before Sunday morning.

We had a good lot of conversations during those days. One thing we realised was that, while at sea, we were no longer in any real control of our lives. Normally, on these sailing trips, if the wind is not strong enough we motor until it is again, or we arrive. But we were on a trip beyond our fuel capacity. So we had no choice but to sit and wait for the wind. We couldn't get off. We couldn't say 'enough of this' and check out. We were there for the duration no matter how long this was. Chris' plane was of no interest to the gods of circumstance. If he didn't catch it then tough. If we ran out of food and water then tough too. It was like taking our comfort zone and dumping it a hundred miles out at sea, literally.

We arrived at Gijon in the early hours of Sunday. A short, but very deep, sleep later we got up to shower, check in with customs, look around and have a breakfast. Chris found his bus and left at lunchtime and I got back to plan my next moves; replenish the boat and replenish myself.

-

It was with mixed feelings that I had said goodbye to Chris. It was nice to have the boat to myself again but I was sorry to lose good company. It was like a friend staying in my living room: fun but inconvenient at the same time. I'd forgotten what good company he was. We'd met last year on a delivery trip from Milford Haven to Brest. So in a way he was doing the next stage of the journey. Perhaps the next trip for him would be to Madeira; an Atlantic circuit in stages? His cooking was wonderful; but what a mess in the galley!

As I got used to the lower costs in Gijon I realised that this journey is a diary of adapting to a change in lifestyle. After the first part of an extended holiday I had to go to a laundry. Then there was the realisation that I was living in a small space. There is the constant moving from place to place and then the loss of control over that movement because of weather. I have exchanged the large house and predictability of everyday living for my travelling world where the weather and immediate environment have more impact than can be ignored.

I have also realised what a good bunch of friends I have. It was good to spend time with my brother; although we live in different worlds I felt a spirit of the way we used to be as kids. Both of us are adventurous spirits but we have not done this together for a long time. Then there are my friends from the Avon Outdoor Activities Club in Bristol. They don't see this journey as anything more than a normal outing. Rob saw me as far as St Ives, Simon in Brittany and Chris over Biscay. All have taken the trip in their stride. And they have stimulated me more than they probably know. These are the sorts of things that we take for granted in everyday life. Once you step outside that, then they become apparent.

In Gijon I started the process of adapting to Spain. After two weeks in France I had regained a lot of my French; now I had to think in Spanish but I kept trying to talk in a mixture. As, in Spanish, I only know the first person and the present tense, my French keeps cutting in. It was hard work going to the market. I almost shied away from buying any food until I realised that I would go hungry unless I did. I suppose it was made harder by not having slept the night before. I had been to a bar where they kept serving a drink which was set on fire before they added cream. I had to try one: it was a variant of Irish coffee. It kept me awake all night.

The weather pattern meant that most of the yachts returning to France left soon after I arrived. There were fewer boats and almost empty pontoons in the marina. My French neighbours have gearbox problem. I could help with that but only in diagnosis. Taking the thing to pieces was beyond my abilities. There were now three UK boats there. I got talking to one; they were on the way back to La Rochelle and could give me local knowledge about the way to La Coruna. They had also crossed the Atlantic several times so could advise me on this too.

The weather was not good for me to continue so I stayed another day in Gijon. It was sunny. I sat in a bar drinking hot chocolate with churros. This is deep fried sticks of batter dipped in a chocolate sauce so thick that it leaves the cup with the churros when you dip it. Life felt good. Then the close humidity was broken by a fresh wind and a burst of rainfall. My home is the wide world when the sun shines but it shrinks to the size of a small boat when it rains. I retreated to my tiny one-bedroom, floating studio apartment and did a few chores, caught up on sleep and cooked. I had just settled down to tea and had some music on when I got a phone call. It was from Ali, a woman who I had fallen for not long before departing. Logically it was silly; to start a relationship just before leaving; but then what part does wisdom play in logic? Or vice versa? Well neither really as she was calling to tell me it was over.

Suddenly I felt lonely. Somehow, the thought of her visiting me at Xmas, and possibly at Easter too, had had a stabilising effect on my year; and then, recently, she had suggested a week in October, when I got to Madeira. I hadn't realised how important this was to me until it was not going to happen. I felt adrift. I went out for a drink. I noticed that I was in a bar where, for the only time since one night in Bilbao, years ago, I saw young people in Spain getting drunk the same way that the Brits do. I had to push past them, like in a pub, to get to my seat. Everyone paid at the bar, which is unusual in Spain. I went back to the boat. On the way I bumped into my French neighbours and joined them for a beer. I was a bit disappointed that they didn't want to go into a bar playing salsa music but, after exploring, we realised that this was the only bar open. Inside there were quite a lot of people shifting themselves, vaguely salsa fashion, but no couples dancing together. What a pity. I had been mentally rehearsing all my moves so that I could have dance. Dancing always ups my spirits. It was too loud to talk, across our languages, inside so we moved outside. A friendly chap got into conversation with us; he was quite charming in his way, for several minutes, until we said we didn't want to buy any cocaine from him. Pouf; he vanished. Meanwhile a fight broke out. I say a fight but it was more a bald-headed bloke looking for a fight and being pushed over. So he took off his shoes and danced down the street. We decided to leave. It was difficult to pay as the staff were sorting out some other trouble with another group outside. When I did get to pay, the beers cost double what they cost elsewhere, and I paid for all three of us. I've come all this way to find drunken aggression, bad dancing, drugs, inflated prices and emotional upset. I went to bed feeling well and truly stung.

I woke nursing a hangover and a bruised ego. I say woke as if it were one event but it happened several times during the night. At home, before bed, when I was drunk, I used to remember: water for hydration, open the window for air, brush my teeth for comfort, and paracetamol for the hangover. I can't open the hatch, it would have let the rain in, and I forgot the paracetamol and water. I've noticed before: that travelling alone I become emotionally labile. It's all too easy to go down and brood with no one to talk it through with. On the other hand I was lifted when my French neighbours noticed and offered me support. Soon the sun was out with the wind and it was a perfect day for making passage to La Coruna. But I'd missed it. I think I got a sort of port fever. I was worried about starting a longish journey on my own; and knowing that there were several sailing days, each with a night on my own. But I had other friends to see and sail with further on; and shortly before Xmas my daughter would be visiting.

I'd been keeping accounts. I was going a bit over budget. Although it was cheaper in Spain I'd been staying in a marina and that bumps up the cost. So I did my washing by hand. It was quite fun to stand outside with two bowls of water and a hose pipe, rinsing a selection of clothes and then hanging them up. The guard rail around the deck and some of the lines make excellent washing lines. I had the boat done up like a dressed ship. I wonder what the crowds on the harbour walls think about me airing my clean laundry in public; or what flag signals I may be sending unintentionally. My English neighbours visited for sundowner drinks. It was nice to chat about boats and places to visit. I'm glad I don't have fancy equipment though. Their fancy autohelm which ties in with all the other navigation equipment had been playing up. Although, eventually sorted out, they had, at one point, been looking at a bill for way over a thousand euros. When my basic electronic tiller pilot went wrong Simon fixed it by taking the back off and putting the drive band back in place.

As I left Gijon, the next day, two things happened. The mountains behind started to rise like ridiculously corny cardboard cut-outs. It was like the scenery in a bad, black and white movie. Then the mists rose as well and they became quite mystical. The other was a deep sense of sadness. Not a depression but a welling up of emotion. There was no wind, the sea was flat and I didn't have the powers to summon a mage wind. Each breath I took would lift up just a bit more emotion. I was a bit scared. I tried to accept it but it took a lot of effort. I wanted it to be like the ending of the first story in the Earthsea trilogy; he turns to the being following him and says: "My name is Ged." I cry when I read that bit; every time.

I shouted: "My name is Matt" as loud as I could. I ranted at the cloudless sky and the no-wind. Three days in port and one day sailing on my own and I'm already losing the plot. What will it be like crossing the Atlantic? I wondered if this was the realisation that this was more than a holiday. This is my life for the year. The theme of Gijon was loss. I'd lost my sailing companions and a relationship. I'd even lost a fender. Now I was on my own. I wondered if this was grief for the world I've left behind; a secure, social and reasonably dependable world. Even now, lying in my bed in Bristol, those feelings stir. I sometimes wish that we could have seen that year out together.

I made a cup of tea and a salami baguette and felt better for all the shouting. But the feelings returned off and on during the next two weeks. This was my first real sail on my own. I motored for several hours, got two hours sailing in, and then motored for the next three. I'd originally thought I'd have to do my first engine service somewhere in the Canaries. Now it looked like I might be doing it in La Coruna. I put the music on very loud. I could hear it in the cockpit; first some classical, which included the Onedin Line theme, and then some salsa - if I couldn't dance at least I could shift me weight about - and then a track of my daughter singing. She's very good and it always makes me good to hear her sing.

In Luarca, along the coast, I couldn't go ashore. The visitors' moorings are bow to against a breakwater. What it doesn't say in the pilot is that, even at high tide, the wall is a precipice, three metres high. You have to tie a line to a buoy from the stern and then motor forward to the wall; stop, hook on a line to a cleat at the top, and then pull back to the stern buoy. "On me tod? You're 'avin a larf!" I told the pilot book. Even with a full complement of crew I'm not sure how we would have tackled it. As I was the only yacht there, I moored between two of the buoys. Because they were too close I rigged up an ingenious way of keeping them from bashing their dirty, rough, steel edges into me. Unfortunately, I forgot to take a photo. I rigged the spinnaker pole, at right angles to the boat from the mast, tied with the mooring line vertical to the buoy. This meant that I was forward of the stern buoy and away to beam from the forward buoy. I wasn't getting the dinghy out for a short visit ashore. I went to bed and was on my way by 8.30 the next day.

There was no wind again. I was sure that I'd heard something about wind in Biscay. When I wrote my journal up that evening I was glad that my passage plan had a built in contingency. Quite by chance, as I was bored with motoring, I changed plan and went to Ribadeo, only twenty five miles on. As I reached the end of the ria, the wind just blew up. It was Force 5 in a matter of minutes and was near gale by midnight. I got the mooring wrong and bumped a pontoon pile in the cross wind; but, as my yachtmaster instructor friend says: better to get it wrong slowly than wrong fast. I wondered if I'd have too much wind the next day. If it was good then two more days and I'd be in La Coruna. Kyle was already there and I would see a friend who lives there. Perhaps he'd let me have a bath.

In Ribadeo the wind increased during the night; the boat was lurching at the end of its moorings. In the morning I had a look around. Ribadeo was, I thought, a typical Spanish town. Not in the sense of being Spanish but in the sense that it could have been a small town in England. It had its pedestrianised area, shops that were obviously part of a high-street chain, various sweet shops, take-aways and bread shops. I felt quite at home. The main difference was that all these people were out perambulating on a Thursday evening. I wondered if this was a holiday town, a holiday or just normal. I had a beer, a tapa and then wandered back to the boat seeing the world with a fuzzy, wonderful glow. I was a bit drunk on one beer. Finding my way down the steep hill to the marina I realised that I needed to sober up before I cooked my supper.

With the wind buffeting it the lurching boat reminded me of a conference I went to a few years ago. The social evening was in a science museum. One of the treats was to go on a flight simulator. They put you in a room which was suspended by hydraulic rams which moved it about to give you the feelings associated with the flight view image on the screen. The trouble was that the projector light broke for the group before me. They had spent ten minutes being thrown around in the dark! They emerged from the experience in some confusion but, immediately turned it into the subject of a drunken discussion. In the boat, in the dark, every now and then I would awake with the world falling away from underneath me; and then it would bounce back fast. As I was waking at strange intervals I would wonder what was happening as the fragments of a dream intertwined with my awakening. I kept forgetting which way around I was in the boat, or even that I was in a boat.

I went up to town again to buy breakfast and food for the next few days in the supermarket I found the day before. I have always been interested in the nature of culture and change. When a patient administration system was put in at the hospital I worked in I was fascinated in the way that my fellow nurses continued to use the admission book. This was now redundant as all the information was on the computer. The justification was that they could use the book to answer telephone queries from community healthcare workers when they had limited access to a computer. So they kept using it for something that was not part of their job.

When I first started nursing we were just introducing the nursing process; a form of management feedback loop involving assessment, planning, intervention and evaluation. It was supposed to change the approach to nursing from task to a holistic attitude. However, what tended to happen was that nurses would think: "what do we do?" and then think of assessments and how to make the plans to fit what they already did. So we filled out loads of paperwork to satisfy the idea while the practice remained the same. The NHS organisation is so large that the cultural momentum is very hard to shift. What chance a single government and their social policy? People will continue on their way; and mea culpa; mea culpa maxima!

The principle behind the supermarket is efficiency and speed. It suits the UK culture of individual space and reserve. We can speed through without communication, check ourselves out and be out of there. It makes me think of the times that I heard people say that they have sat in a bar or cafe on their own while all the rest of the bar is in conversation. We have to be introduced – so English! In Spain this doesn't appear to be part of the culture. Everything seems to be based around a social perspective. Strangers have multi-part conversations on the bus, in the cafe, from table to table in restaurants, when I ask directions, all the time. One of my friends near Valencia once remarked that, in Spain, two is a conversation, three is a shouting match. To go shopping and not talk is just done. The normal markets are still a big thing. What chance have the supermarkets got against this? So they seem to have arrived at what I've heard called the theatre of shopping. In England we put someone in a hat and an apron, stick them behind a self-service meat counter, and they become a butcher. It's a costume. Here, in Ribadeo they arrange the fruit section, the fish section and the meat section etc in to little market stalls. And we queue to buy things from them. OK I can choose my fruit but I still have to have the assistant weigh it and price it. So I queued for my fish, my meat, my fruit and then to pay. It all is supermarket produce but it gives the impression of an ordinary market – to a degree.

My German neighbour helped me to slip moorings as the

wind was still strong. Coming out of the river entrance it looked like I was going to have a nice beam reach down the coast. But that was only an appearance; the wind was being funneled down the valley. It was nearly on the nose as I got out to sea. It abated shortly after that so, waiting twenty minutes, I shook the reefs out. Another twenty minutes I was happily moving to windward so I went and did some chores below. All was good. I had a rest on a bunk. And then she hove to. Mildred is pretty good but she does have a problem with wind changes. This was a big change. I had to get her back on track and take some reefs in again as the wind got up again. Not only that but the sea was now jumping the boat around. Going from relaxation to this so quickly was quite scary. I'm not yet used to this fairground ride on my own; there's always a thought that I might trip and go overboard. Even with a safety line on I would still be hard pressed to pull myself back on board in this kind of choppy sea. Back on course I sailed for a few hours but realised I needed to motor to get to a destination before dark. With the wind on the nose I had not been going very far even though travelling at some speed.

It was dark, though, by the time I reached the Ria Barquero. It was an odd feeling to be motoring up to a beach. I could hear the surf breaking in little waves but I couldn't see it. It was only about 100 metres away. Having checked the tide times and heights I was happy that I was in a good place, the anchor was holding and I was quietly in the lee of the headland. I made my supper and settled down to a good sleep. Three hours later the wind change, promised for twelve hours ago, had finally happened; but not as forecast to variable light winds. It was a strong NW wind straight down the ria and on to us. We were bucking and snatching at the anchor chain. There was a loud snap as the boat rose and tried to take the chain upwards each time a wave rolled us up. I let out more chain but it was no good. I set up a snubber; a length of nylon rope that takes the elastic place of the last few metres of chain. At three in the morning, on a rolling boat, I was half naked, fiddling about with bits of shackle, chain and rope in the dark. What a life. I went back to bed but it was like being in the flight simulator again.

I'd had enough by eight o'clock. I had breakfast, made a passage plan and set off. I started at nine but by the time I'd hauled in all that anchor chain, while trying to set George to steer against the strong wind away from the lee shore, and being splashed with salty water, it was ten o'clock by the time I left the ria. It's referred to as a delightful ria in the pilot; it's a pity I didn't get to see any of it.

I got the sails up with two reefs in and off we set. We were racing along at over six knots or about eight miles per hour. We rounded the headland and then on to a run. The wind was almost right behind so there is no balance to stop the boat rolling from side to side. I changed course slightly and that was a bit better. It was slightly longer but more comfortable. That was it for eight hours apart from gybing three times to keep the course. Gybing is potentially dangerous in high winds so extra care is needed. The sail comes across from one side to the other very fast; anything in its way will simply go with it, be that bits of rigging, stuff caught on the deck or my head. That would be it: overboard and unconscious while Mildred steers the boat on.

We were surfing three to four metre waves, rolling crests, one after each other. I was standing in the cockpit looking forward over the front of the boat into valleys up to six metres below; and over we'd go. Mildred was constant; she kept us on course with only the odd variation but never anywhere near an accidental gybe. After I got used to it I started to relax. I even got my head down for the odd ten minute spell. It was good fun but quite tiring and a little scary so it was good to get some rest.

The thing about longer journeys is that, unlike short ones, you can't make do until you get to shore. With a little day hop in strong winds you can stay up on deck and be hungry until you get there. With the four day Biscay crossing we'd had to get into a routine. Now, on my own, I knew I had to eat something substantial before I got to La Coruna. I'd had a big breakfast before leaving, but all that anchor work gave me another hunger so I'd eaten all the pain au chocolate by lunch where I'd had my usual cheese and meat baguettes. Now I needed something to see me through the last hour or two. Suddenly I thought: there was some ordinary bread left plus some peanut butter and honey that I'd packed from home. Oh yes, comfort food and full of calories.

About two hours away from my destination I heard some English voices on the radio discussing the marina in La Coruna. One of them was already there so I called them to ask them to let the marineros know that I was arriving soon. I heard no more but, as I rounded the breakwater, they were waiting for me. They guided me in and helped me secure the boat in the high winds. After six or so hours sleep in the last two nights, fifty five miles today over eleven hours, I was exhausted. They looked at me, saw this and, offering me the key to the showers, said to come up and sort the paperwork in the morning.

Kyle and his friend Jose arrived shortly after. They left while I went to wash all the salt water off, shave and shower. What a wonderful feeling. I joined them in a bar in town with another friend of Jose's. We had some tapas, a drink and then I was all in. I went back to the boat for my first real sleep for what seemed a very long time.

The next day was a day of rest for me. I suddenly realised that this was the Sunday of August Bank Holiday weekend. If I'd been back in Blighty I would have probably been chilling on a Cornish beach, perhaps in the sea. As it was, I was watching a feral cat in the blindingly bright sunshine on the massive stones of the breakwater. It was a light brown colour, camouflaged against the stained stones and seaweed. It was the most fox-like cat I have ever seen; but also lionesque. At this distance it appeared to have rippling muscles under its taught skin. It was slinking down to the water, all concentration, to explore the gaps between the stones. There was an air of predator about it; the way it slid over the top of a rock and into the hole beyond with purpose, searching for something unseen to me. Up above people were walking past oblivious. It continued below the level of the pavement, unconcerned.

Then it stopped, washed and looked about itself. It was like the stoning scene in The Life of Brian. Was anyone slinking? No, no,no...who me? Then she squatted down to wee on a piece of seaweed and wandered off. I don't know why but it made me feel good to see this little cameo role. I smiled and went back to my coffee and notes.

Not long later and old acquaintance dropped by. The cruise liner P&O Oriana was in town. A few years ago, as a flight nurse, I had repatriated a patient from her in Tenerife. The crew had been very nice to me. They'd shown me around all her concentrated fun factory, the crew's dining room and the hospital. I'd been fed and entertained while I waited for the flight home with my patient. I was welcomed as a visitor in her own enormous world. Now she was visiting my little world. Actually, I doubt that anyone on board noticed Safe Arrival sitting in the marina.

One thing about La Coruna is that the approach to it from the sea, and the headland (it is a promontory) is dominated by a large square lighthouse. It's one of those entities that cannot be mentioned without an explanatory description. It is the Torres de Hercules lighthouse – but this has to be followed by: it is the oldest working lighthouse in the world – built by the Romans. So be prepared to hear this phrase, or equivalent, many times.

Back in June I had been wandering around the Dylan Thomas

museum in Swansea. One of the notable things was that he found it difficult to write in cities. His time in London and New York were barren times for his writing. Catatonia echoed this with their song about London sucking the life out of them. I have found, in my lesser way, the same thing about La Coruna. I just stopped taking any notes. I thought about it but couldn't do more than that. It was just too much bother. It's a busy city. It's a big fish at the corner of rural Spain. I was told about an expression that translates literally as: people in Coruna live life out of the gallery. There is an element of attempted Parisian lifestyle. In one part near the docks the outdoor seats to the restaurants all sit facing outwards. The occupants are all well-heeled, middle aged women with articulate make-up. The windows to the apartments above are not the usual 'closed to the outside' but big glass, designed to be visible from outside. Elsewhere the rest of the city got on with its own life. I liked La Coruna. It had a life of its own, a character.

I met my friend who lives there. I first met Dave on a Brittany sailing week a couple of years ago. It was his first time on a yacht and I was impressed, and slightly envious, of his complete lack of seasickness. Far more important though was that he quickly realised that the crew was made up of non-foodies. The first shopping trip had resulted in the cheapest and blandest menu possible. It was completely devoid of any fun; simply a refueling system. On the second day Dave had offered to look after the cooking. That was it; he was a friend for life; and what a cook he was. He could make delicious meals out of almost anything. Crossing back from Alderney to Fowey in a Force 7 he was happily cooking up a hot meal while the boat rolled over the waves.

He had wanted to join me in some of the trip but, having just started a family, his time was occupied by fatherhood and coping with the recession. He was a great help though. He got the bit between his teeth about sorting out my boat. He took a cabin door off and fixed it, he cut me a mirror, he made a panel to cover the back of the depth gauge and he made up an infill to make a double bed out of the saloon seats. However, the big challenge was to find a solenoid valve for the gas cooker. We drove all over La Coruna. We got to know all the different trading estates and the types and words for gas solenoid. It was like a competition that I've heard about for hardware store assistants. The object is to ask more and more specific questions until the customer cannot answer and has to leave empty handed. You ask for some 1in screws.

"8s or 10s sir?"

"8s"

"Steel or brass sir?"

"Steel"

"Galvanised or stainless sir? "Cross head or slot?" countersunk or raised? Etc.

Every time that we thought that we'd got the questions sorted the next place would add a further question. Dave would turn to me and translate' and the process would start again. I could only grab the odd gist of the conversations between Dave and the counter assistants but I got the idea when he had to turn and ask me each time. We got so close. In one place we found one but it was an enormous industrial thing for massive fittings. It would have served in factory heating system well. In another we found exactly what I was looking for – except that it was twenty four volt. Safe Arrival is twelve volt.

One day we went out for lunch in a restaurant run by one of his relatives. The owner had been a fisherman previously and so knew all the fish market people and got the best stuff. The meal started ordinarily enough. We had a beer and a tapa; a sardine on a potato bed. Then the prawns arrived. We tucked in, stripping off the heads and coverings. Then the crab arrived. By this time my plate resembled a dustbin with all the prawn remnants and the paper towels I had wiped my fingers with. But add to this then the crab shells. In the UK crabs come with implements to open them. I've always thought they look like eyelash curlers. Here we used our teeth and the knife. We stabbed open the joints and prised out little pieces of meat. The shells themselves were filled with other meat in a sauce. It was so rich that I could only eat two before having to rest. Then they brought another plate. Dave just kept eating. How did he do this? Meanwhile his wife, Velen wandered about chatting to other members of her family. I love this about Spain: in the UK eating is a fussy business with all sorts of social constrictions. It's getting better but is still so uptight compared with here. A paper table cloth was being increasingly covered in bits of waste food. Our plates were piled high with the inedible bits of seafood and everyone came and chatted with us. It's a social affair.

The next course looked like it had arrived from a Star Wars movie. Goose barnacles look like they are made out of latex with little claws at the end of their rubbery legs. I couldn't resist getting a four-legged one to walk about my plate while exclaiming "Eat me not will you now!" Yoda, eat your heart out. Velen and I got through a few but Dave just went on eating. We laughed and I pointed to her flat stomach (after having recently had a baby) and his less-flat one. "Ahora, se por que!" It was not correct Spanish but it made sense to her.

The marina at La Coruna is a major stopping place for boat either on the way north to, or south from, Biscay. So there are all nationalities there on real cruising yachts. Mine was very small in comparison with most of them. When I went to say thanks to the guy, Lee, who I'd spoken to on the radio I was introduced to his boat owner Harkan. Harkan, Swedish, was a larger than life character. He had a confidence, an arrogance, that I would not want to get on the wrong side of. I could tell that he made things happen. And one night he was in the mood to have fun. Kyle had just announced his decision to pull out of crewing with me and I was not relishing the trip around the Finisterre on my own. So when we went for a sundowner I joined these two in the bar. They were in conversation with three other Swedes who had arrived that afternoon from Scilly, as part of a world circumnavigation. Harkan suggested a meal out. They were all tired and hungry and, like me, relished the idea of a night out.

The three were a brother and sister and their friend. The sister sat at the end of the table while all us blokes lined up each side. She seemed quite aware of the power of her beauty and youth. Harkan ordered about four bottles of wine and we got stuck into a dual language set of conversations. It was a bit odd eating Italian in Spain but there you go. Half way (or at least some time) through the evening I saw Harkan try to whisper something to the waiter. He was quite drunk and it looked like a stage whisper; it was conspiratorial like the baddy in a pantomime. He had a reasonable grasp of Spanish, better than mine, but what he lacked in ability he made up for in drunken confidence. I think the waiter quite enjoyed the conversation.

A short while later, the room darkened slightly, a horrible happy birthday song came on and the waiters all marched in with a sparkler pricked pudding. They made for the sister who looked a bit surprised and pointed at her brother. So they gave it to him. Harkan's plot had been to pretend that it was her birthday and get a treat for her. Quite by chance it happened to be her brother's birthday. So he got his cake and we all clapped and sang along with the song. That's probably one of those things that is hilarious when drunk and not really funny at all.

When we finally left we got back to the marina and went to Harkan's boat where we drank punch. That was a mistake. That led to a hangover-induced second day of rest. I missed Lee and Harkan when they left. Harkan was a social glue. Lee was generous, helpful and gave me some fishing gear. He had paid the bill at the restaurant for all of us.

With Kyle pulling out there was no hurry for me to move now. In some ways this was good. It meant I could relax and sort the maintenance out more thoroughly. On the other hand it was a problem. I got port fever. I realised that I was scared of moving on. I didn't want to do this on my own. I didn't want to be lonely in anchorages. I wanted to share this with others. I was starting to get my head around what I'd taken on; and starting to think what I wanted from it; and seeing if I could square the two.

I left the estuary at La Coruna with some trepidation. I knew I needed to get going but I was worried about Finisterre's reputation and about how I would handle it. I rounded Torre de Hercules (that's the oldest working lighthouse in the world – built by the Romans) and started to think about the day ready to put some sort of plan in place. It's hard work getting a boat away from a marina on your own; so I needed a second breakfast. It's probably partly the stress as much as the work. I was motoring again as the wind was light. I headed west to round the last corner of Spain and down the Cost de Morte. Several hours later I could still see Torre de Hercules (etc.) It reminded me of a few years ago when I had been on a boat with friends in Scilly. It was a sailing school boat, not kitted out for passages, with an engine the power of a dinghy outboard. At full revs it just got to four knots. Motoring back to Falmouth we had the Lizard lighthouse in sight for over eight hours! At last the Torre de Hercules (etc) disappeared.

During the day I alternated between eating, resting, dreaming and navigation. I knew the weather was going to close in at some point in the next few days so, when I realised that I'd made good time, I missed out the first anchorage and went on to Camarinas, a small town in a little ria. The rias around the north west coast of Spain are like Scottish Lochs. They can stretch fourteen miles inland. They are often protected from the Atlantic swells by small, rocky islands across their mouths. The navigation in is a little tricky but nothing treacherous. As I tied up I heard "Hiya" from behind me. Barry and Anne, from Bolton, welcomed me in. I joined them in a bar for a beer once I'd put the boat to bed. They were in a twenty one foot homemade yacht; they were doing the same circuit as me and had been caught in a Force 8 plus across Biscay. "What did you do" I asked. "Oh we just hove to." was the reply. Respect. Nearing port their motor had a cooling problem. For the last few hours they had been pouring sea water over the heat exchanger and bailing it out as they went. More respect.

I slept well that night except at midnight when they set off the firecrackers across the bay. I went for a long walk the next morning. I rounded the headland and along the coast. I was looking for what Dave had called the 'English Graveyard.' This is a burial ground for a ship of English people who were killed when their ship was blown on to the coast here. Because they were not Catholic they could not be buried in the normal graveyards; so the locals had made one just for them. I didn't see any but, apparently, it is not uncommon to find ordinary gardens with a grave dug for a single sailor found washed up on the shore. I found the story quite touching; it shows that people will care for each other across fundamental ideological boundaries.

I had lunch sitting in the shade, looking across the sea, past the wind farms, to the horizon. Once again, I'd taken a day off when the wind was perfect for my journey, but I wasn't worried. I was beginning, very slightly, to come to terms with solitary life. Although only slight, the change was comforting. I sat there eating baguettes with jamon, tomate and olive oil. An old friend who lives near Valencia had introduced me to these a couple of years ago. They are so simple and yet so good to eat on a walk. Sitting there, I remembered the scene in Shawshank Redemption when he finds the rock that has no business being there in that wall in that field. He looks around; there is no sound except for the wind and the creatures in the field. Like him, all I could hear was the sea and the wind and a few insects in the warm sunshine. It was very peaceful. I dozed off. I didn't find the graveyard.

Having missed the wind from that day, I motored most of the way to a small town in Ria Muros. I ticked another box in my bucket list in rounding Finisterre. It was only just visible when I came down the west side. The air was so wet that, as the wind blew up and over it, the moisture was released into a veil-like cloud. It hugged the silhouette over the top forming a helmet like Darth Vader's. Unfortunately, this wind was bang on the nose for me. A few miles further south and I was in clear sunshine. That's how quickly the weather can change along this coast.

I had realised that I needed some emotional grounding so I phoned a couple of friends. They were very helpful and suggested ways that I could approach my feelings. Between them I began to realise that there were questions that I needed to answer. To answer these I needed to get away from the boat and the sea. So I planned that, after Hazel's visit, I would go home to Bristol for a week to stay with some friends. There I would decide what to do; to call off the trip, to modify it or to carry on. Somehow, after making this realisation, I felt much calmer and relaxed. I slept in that morning quite happily listening to music and reading. I was staying in Portosin, way up one Ria Muros, for a few days. I had nothing pressing to do except check busses to Santiago. There were nice walks about and the squally rain was due to abate. I met Barry in a bar and we got drunk together. Life was back on course. It may not have been the course I planned but, hey, I could change course to avoid the squalls.

I stayed in Portosin for four nights. I was due to meet Hazel at the airport in Santiago and the busses went from there regularly so it was an easy place to stop. Stuart, another single hander, arrived one morning. We had a discussion about issues to face single handed. Then John and Maggie on a boat called Lazy Pelican arrived. All these three had been driven in to the marina by the bad weather. That night they had drinks party on Lazy P. We all arrived, already a little tipsy, to eat tapas and further drinks. I wondered during the evening about these short-lived friendships along the way. In some way it reminded me of my first week or two at university; we have no shared experiences so all the talk has to be about what we have done before. I had a silly thought. I wanted to know how they would, if they were estate agents and the pope wanted to sell, describe the Vatican in the shop front blurb. (A grey-smoke feature, puppets on guard etc) That's not my idea; it's from a conversation I once had with two friends in Bristol whilst out drinking. The point is that I wanted to find out how these people thought and how they could be funny in the moment; not just to recount funny stories. I had wanted company, but at what price?

I went for a walk in the hills. It was very like Scotland there; pine and hills with inland sea-lakes. The weather was similar too. It went from rainy to hot sun and back a couple of times during the five hours I was out. It was good to get some exercise again. I saw these hills again from the bus the next day on the way to meet Hazel in Santiago de Compostela. The busses are very good but I had settled into such a relaxed way of life that I forgot to think about getting off. I passed a stop where lots of people got off before I wondered if this was my stop too. Slightly anxious, I couldn't understand the thick Galician dialect of the driver but a fellow passenger explained that we were going to the bus station. It turned out that the road works meant the bus was now routed nearer the centre than the terminus;

that's why they'd all got off. Another change and I was at the airport. It was a long time since things had travelled this fast. In La Coruna, Dave had driven me faster than I'd been for over a month but I could talk with him and understood where I was going. On the bus I couldn't; and then airplanes travel so much faster. I sat there, in the airport, reading Pride and Prejudice; it seemed to be easier to read about coaches and horses than face up to the speed of aircraft.

5 ATLANTIC SPAIN: STABILITY

I am sitting in Porto again. It is exactly two weeks after my first visit. Then, we had rushed around, hot, depositing bags in left luggage, without much time to relax before heading to the airport. This time I had a whole day, it was cooler, I knew where a lot of things were and I had a packed lunch. I sat in the same cafe near the station that we had sat before and thought about the difference. Then I had been about to return the Bristol, unsure if I were going to continue the journey. Now I was relaxed, confident in the rest of the year and, despite being alone, enjoying walking around. It occurred to me that a lot of water had passed under the bridge but no sea under the boat. A week seeing friends in Bristol, talking over issues, had sorted me out. And I'd been hit by a sense of proportion: two friends had serious problems. Mine were insignificant in comparison. That's the trouble with navel gazing; the navel can become the whole world.

Hazel and I had wandered around Santiago. I had first met her at university in Norwich. At one point we'd had a short relationship. Not long after, when I moved to Bristol, we lost touch. A couple of years ago I bumped into her at a festival. Apart from some minor signs of aging she hadn't really changed at all. We swapped life stories and became friends again. She'd also joined me when we took Safe Arrival out for sea trials in the Bristol Channel. It was lovely to see her at the airport. She was a reminder of good things.

The first thing I noticed about Santiago is the number of walkers and how many of them are limping or hobbling; the nearer to the cathedral the more there are. They vary in the gear they carry enormously. Some are in full walking outfits not out of place in the Alps. Others are in capes, carrying ostentatious staves; some are in fully worn out boots while some appear to have walked out of Harrods that morning. It turns out that there are varying levels of support for walkers on the Camino. So some do it all unassisted while others have anything from someone to carry their tent through to those who have everything done for them bar the walking. They also start from different stages along the route.

I can't talk. I bagged my first Munroe with the aid of the train up Cairngorm. I remember all the notices about not walking around the mountain up there because of the damage to the environment. The eight of us stood, stationed around the compound, like stooges from The Great Escape. Once we'd all nodded that it was safe we opened the gate and walked out fast but not so fast that we attracted attention. It was no problem as we walked up the stone path until far away and we could set off for our destination without worrying about over-walking the fauna. But I could not claim it as a real Munroe.

By the cathedral we saw an enormous queue. They were waiting to hug the stone. Around the back we found a short one for looking around the cathedral. They had electric candles. You put ten cents in and one model candle would flash an LED for a few seconds to let you know which one was yours and then it would 'burn' for ten minutes. Was this efficiency or health and safety I wondered. The incense burner for use during masses was massive. It was suspended, pendulum like, on a line, high above the pews. Apparently, during mass, the priest swings it across the congregation. I had this irreverent thought: what if there was a rugby club in the congregation? Would they perform a line out lift for one them to jump up and grab it in the air?

We had lunch out and then got back to the boat. After the wind and rain of the last few days it broke sunny; only for a mist to blow in. We had to spend another night in Portosin.

I had received several emails of support during the previous week. That was good. I let them ferment in the back of my mind. It got me thinking about how technology has affected travel. The book that had inspired me to do this was written at the beginning of the nineties. John Beattie had no internet, no GPS and no mobile phone. Every time he checked in to a port he had to buy a phone card and find a phone box before he could ring home. I could phone practically at any time. If he got lost he had to rely on the sun and his sextant sighting abilities. I could have a quick check on the GPS. Mine was a very basic GPS; other voyagers I had met had large screen chart plotters with all the charts and other information too. I knew where I was by transferring the coordinates on to a paper chart. I did have a sextant but had not got around to using it. I was waiting for the open sea. Others also had satellite phones where they could connect to the internet at any time. I had to find wi-fi in marinas or in cafes. I didn't mind as it gave me an excuse to have a coffee.

The effect of this technology was to shrink and expand my sense of the size of the world. It shrank in that I was hundreds of miles from home and yet I knew what was going on there through social media. I was using my work email so I still got a few work emails (instantly deleted.) I had the sense that I was still there in some part. My sense of expanded world came from the understanding of how much I used to pack into each day. In travelling, the pressing things to do are more concerned with vagaries of the weather. Otherwise, I could spend two hours shopping for food; or a morning in a cafe. I had vague plans on how to meet people in arranged places but I had given myself plenty of leeway on times. I was living in the spaces that I didn't normally have. At first those spaces seemed too big to comprehend. I felt that I was living in the gaps between the paving stones. Sometimes I panicked at the loss of grounding. At other times I felt quite comfortable with it. Sometimes I wanted to share the world of home that I glimpsed through the internet; a bit of homesickness.

One day Barry, ex-navy, used to being away for long times, told me that I had to remember that it was me that had left. A week to us, with no routine, is a long time whereas the routine of going to work every week has two effects: firstly it rushes time past so that a week seems a comparatively short time. Secondly, there is a tendency for anyone who isn't around to slowly fade into the background. I'd moved away and was now fading in their minds. I realised, too, that it was likely that time would speed up the nearer I got to the end of the trip. That's like the first week of a two-week holiday lasting forever and the second week whizzing past. I wondered if this was this what people had meant when they said I would learn about myself.

At last the sun came out and the northerly wind appeared. We set off out of Portosin towards the next ria and an anchorage outside San Vincente. It was a pity but we had to miss out Ria Arusa. It is supposed to be lovely but it involved some tricky navigation and I didn't have the large scale chart. I always knew that I was going to miss bits out of the trip so I wasn't too unhappy about it. Anyway, I could look in there on the next time around.

San Vincente turned out to be a resort. We had a lovely anchorage off the beach but were too tired to go ashore that night. In the late morning we got the dinghy out and went ashore. After a while we realised that every direction led into yet another holiday villa style residential street. There were no indications of shops or town centre; it was a resort. We found a cafe; the coffee was weak, frothy and served in branded cups. It summed up the town: a disappointment. So we set sail for Cambarro.

In light winds we crossed over into Ria Pontevedra. As we were making such slow progress we altered course. As the predicted northerly wind had turned west we anchored outside a little town of Beuu. It was hot and the water was clear so we went for a swim, my first from Safe Arrival. It was lovely and cool to be in the water after a hot day in the sun.

There is an oft quoted fact that most accidents in yachting happen on the way back from shore in the dinghy. I reflected on this as we approached the ladder. After two beers on an empty stomach I was quite tipsy. The wind had, finally, gone north and got up. The yacht was bucking in rolling sea and we were tipping about in it. I was drunk, with no life jacket, and approaching five tons of jumping plastic. Then, once aboard, the anchor started snatching. Just like last time I had to get out in the night to put a snubber in; and, just like last time, it took an hour to get it all up in the morning.

The poor sleep and effort of weighing anchor was worth it though as we had a lovely sail down to Ria Vigo next day. There is obviously more money in this area. Dave had told me about the lost generation here. Many of the young locals here used to be involved in tobacco and alcohol smuggling. With local knowledge they could come ashore at places that others couldn't. It must have been like the Cornwall of Daphne du Maurier's stories. But then the smuggling had turned to hard drugs and the locals were paid in kind. As addiction spread and took hold the young generation was decimated. So a whole generation was lost. It's a sad story. I hoped it stood as a reminder to others and so had some good to it.

Cangas, our stop for the night, was also a holiday area but in an old fishing village. The main drag was obviously the posing street. We sat outside a cafe watching the very well dressed, sitting to be observed, while the same guy drove past in his flashy car at least three times. It could have been named the city of dogs, as in: Los Perros. Everywhere we looked there was a dog. Some were toy dogs being carried or pulled along the pavement on the end of leads. Others were lugubrious retrievers sitting to attention, hoping that something good was going to happen soon. One poodle/spaniel cross watched excitedly from a balcony above our bar. It would run in and out of its room every time any change happened. As this was a street where people came and went it was constantly on the move. One dog was being carried in a buggy, in the tray under the toddler. The one that got me was the one that sat in the driver's seat (UK) and looked back over its shoulder as it reversed into a pavement menu sign. It wasn't satisfied with knocking it over though. It seemed to call up its friend as a couple of minutes later another car reversed in to run the sign over. Weeing on them isn't good enough any more; dogs have to run street furniture over.

I was surprised how expensive this ramshackle marina was. The showers were dilapidated although they worked well. They were open plan and one head was around a corner facing in. I had turned the two corner ones in and made it into a sort of wet room. It was good to find small pleasures in unusual places. Once we got over the price, we set course for Baiona. This is not far if you go via the Canal de Porta. For all its name this is essentially a gap between the rocky headland and the nearest small island/rock out of the line of rocks that stick out from it. About 100 metres wide it has an underwater island in the middle of the channel. At the shallowest it is easily deep enough to sail over but, as the depth gauge reduced rapidly, I still had a bit of anxiety; what if I had it just a bit wrong?

We had planned to stay in Baiona just for one night and then go down to Porto, but we arrived to find loads of Brits and Norwegians. As Hazel speaks Norg she stopped to talk with them while I chatted to some Brits. The community of the voyagers was becoming clearer. Already there were Barry and Ann plus some others I had been told about. Stuart was in the next marina down the coast. We discovered that this is a beautiful town with lots to see so we decided to stay here for the next day too. Besides, I had managed to separate the water tank filler hose from the top of the flexible tank so I need time to work out how to fix it. It's weird how things came out of the blue. I had never expected this type of maintenance. All I'd done was to fill the tank but somehow the pressure had been too much and it had leaked all over the place. At least the cushions would dry in the sun.

We went to the fort to look over the town and the bay. We had our most expensive coffee yet in the hotel terrace bar surrounded by very well heeled guests. I heard my first American accent since leaving Bristol. That was not quite true as some of the marina staff speak English with an American accent; but this was a real American.

Later a Nicholson 55 sailed in. It was obviously a military boat, flying a blue ensign and crewed by short-haired, fit young men. I was watching them get ready to go the next day when I heard the skipper call an instruction. I knew that voice; it was Rab. I had last seen him when we sailed into the town of Rab, on the island of Rab, in Croatia, on one of our club sailing trips. He'd had difficulty adjusting to a civilian crew and had never been back to sail with us again. I went and said hello. It was quite fun to see him trying to work out who I was. After all, with my best posh voice I could possibly be admiralty brass. I got to wonder about chaos theory when I was in these situations. How many people were there, that I know, sailing around the world; how many of them were nearby; and how many would I actually meet. Or would we just pass in the night.

On the way into the marina we had been going to moor up behind a boat called Ocean Warrior. There is a class of boat called the Warrior but she didn't look like one. As we passed – having been told to moor elsewhere by the marinero - I got into a short conversation with the woman on board. Their maintenance problem dwarfed mine; their engine had bust and they were waiting for a complete replacement. When I went to finish the conversation they invited me onboard for a beer. One beer led to two and then a glass of wine for Hazel when she came back from a shower. Then they produced tapas and slowly the notion of cooking a meal on Safe Arrival was removed from that night. To repay their hospitality I fetched my bottle of Dalwhiney. I have noticed, over the years, that a bottle of fine spirits works wonders in the bonhomie department. A few years earlier, in Cuba, with a girlfriend, I had been staying with a family in their guesthouse when we produced a bottle of rum. At first we had to offer a glass and the first refill. The second refill they had asked if it was OK but after that they helped themselves. I think we learnt more about Cuba, from the inside, from their loosened tongues, on that night than in the whole of the rest of the three weeks there.

The problem with the whisky was that we had to wake up early the next morning to set sail for Porto. With a thick head – only partially thinned by a shower – we motored out of Baiona and down the coast to Portugal. The coast is rocky with high cliffs all the way south to Portugal before it turns into a beach, hundreds of miles long, down to the Algarve. But as we were in poor visibility and could only see the water for a few hundred metres around the boat I have to say that that information came from the pilot book. I was working from ded reckoning and the GPS. Deduced as in: we were here and have been travelling at this speed in this direction so now we should be here. Deduced or not I saw nothing of the coast for almost the whole day.

Poada de Vazim is an unusual marina. It is about fifteen kilometres north of Porto on the end of the metro. It was wonderfully ramshackle with plenty of boats on the hard in various states of repair – or intended repair. The launderette was a room with a couple of domestic washing machines with a pack of powder. To pay you had to wander down to another building across the yard and find the office. What a change from the usual coin operated machinations. Gordon lived there for the summer and taught sailing in the Solent during the winter. He told us that some people were trapped in Vazim; they'd run out of money so couldn't afford to move on. It was cheap and they could just survive but not pay the higher prices either way along the coast. In the night a siren went off. It was to warn boats of poor visibility. Intermittently, it would start up again. Every time it was painful; it would break into my sleep and force me to wake. I lay tortured, waiting for it to repeat, only to fall to sleep again.

Porto was magnificent the next day. It was like Bristol being built around the suspension bridge. We walked across the dual level bridge. The cars cross at river level while pedestrians share the high level with the trams. There really was nothing in between the pavement and the tram lines. The railings were at waist height so we could lean over and look straight down about 100 metres. I had this worry that the trams might knock my feet and tip me over. There was a little bit of breeze to temper the searing sunshine. On one side there were all the port warehouses with gigantic lettering like the Hollywood sign; but the extraordinary view is of the medieval town, hanging down the side of the gorge underneath. It is built on what must be a one in three gradient. It is also a fairly poor area; all the houses are dilapidated; the washing hangs out over the disintegrating balconies the cats and dogs snuffle about in the tiny, steep streets. At the bottom the tourist boats are moored along the river. The pavement is wide with lines of market stalls outside the shops and bars. While we were there Rapid Vienna were playing. The riverside was full of green and white clad, German speaking supporters. One group were singing in a bar; a vanload of police were hanging about close by looking a bit bemused. I'm not sure they were used to this type of supporter behaviour. We spent the day being tourists. Hazel took over the navigation as she steered us around this wonderful city. In the, at last, cooling, evening sunshine we collected the luggage from the station and made our way back to the metro. Our next stop was the airport. I said goodbye to Hazel in the departure lounge; she was going to Stanstead and I to Bristol.

6 LEAVING EUROPE: A NEW CHALLENGE

I sat in another Porto; this time it was Porto Santo, an island off the coast of Madeira. It is the favourite, first port of call on the passage from Portugal. I am finding, after each change or challenge on this journey, that I need to retreat from company and let it all sink in. It's good to sit in a cafe where I don't understand the language and let my thoughts roam back to over the last few weeks.

I'd found it exhausting being back in Bristol. The spaces in time that I was beginning to get used to had been tightened up again. I'd worked out, while talking it over with friends, that I would know if I wanted to go on with the journey once I'd taken a break from it. In Bristol we'd talked over all the options and I'd got the point where I knew I wanted to go on but I was still scared of it. I was still in Bristol. I knew I had to be back on the boat to really know; to be sure.

The flight back left late in the evening. Changing trains from the airport to Povoa de Vazim I sat on the lonely platform, back in a mild climate, for my last train, in an immense silence, surrounded by the peripheral , distant noises of civilisation. Way past midnight, clutching my large box of spares, I found the marina and, stepped on to the boat. As I did so relief flooded through me; all the thinking and wondering and contingency planning was over. I felt like a party balloon deflated; I was still apprehensive but the decision was done. Relaxed at last, I slept well that night. The siren, signaling poor entrance to the marina, went off that night but I was now immune to its sound. I could sleep through it.

I got up early, realising that I had to restock. While shopping in different countries I'd been travelling down my language abilities: fluent in English, reasonable in French, passable in Spanish and now completely lost in Portuguese. This was not helped by a trip to the fish market. I chose an empty counter and then realised why. The woman was irritated that I'd chosen her; grumpy was not really the word. She shouted something to me when I pointed at a sea bream. I didn't understand so she shouted again. Two women on other counters smiled condolence at me. Eventually it transpired that it cost six euro per kilogramme. That was about two euro for a big fish. I smiled and nodded whereat she attacked it with a scaler and a knife. I was beginning to enjoy myself so I asked if I could have some ice to go with it. After all, I don't have a fridge. So now she had to try and understand me. The other stall women behind her were laughing now. They could see me getting my own back. The ice was free, I think, because she was happy to see the back of me.

Back at the marina I was glad to see Barry and Anne again. They were off that afternoon to the Canaries. The wind was strong and from the north; perfect for travelling the eight days south. They had a rousing departure crowd wishing them well. I emailed them the photos I took straight away.

This marina is popular with Brits. There was quite a community. The marina manager laid on a minibus to go to the hypermarket once a week; there was a meal out once a week and a BBQ on Sundays. It was all bring your own but a regular meeting where news was swopped and people introduced to each other. I learnt there about the drugs boat. I'd idly told them that, while I'd been in the UK, I'd read about a yacht being seized with drugs on board off the coast of Portugal. It turned out it had been in that very marina. After the arrest the police had publicised that they had removed so many kilos of heroin. Whoever had organised the trafficking had obviously read this and realised that the police had missed a lot of the drugs. They had taken the night watchman at gunpoint to the boat and smashed their way to the rest of the drugs. Consequently, having a large dash of egg on their face, the customs were taking a lot of interest in all boats after that.

In this travelling world of yotties the constant movement leads to ephemeral friendships. However, the normal formality of slow start, introductions, has to be bypassed. We don't have time to take time. I am invited into practically total strangers' homes and invite them back. We swop stories, information, tools, food and advice. We all had all day; we didn't have to get anywhere in particular and so we chatted, drank coffee, cooked and drank sundowners together.

We learned about the world of sailing together. I was surprised to find that I knew quite a lot about it that others didn't. I thought that I'd be the newbie at this but there were plenty who had less experience and knew less than me about various aspects of sailing. Someone recently described me as having a Velcro mind. I pick up bits of information that stick in my mind. This meant that I would read, in Nigel Caulder's boat owning bible, that anchor windlasses worked in a various ways. I'd absorb this, service my windlass and be able to talk about windlasses (oh such exciting subjects.) that night. And then I'd find that I was the expert. I'd help someone service theirs the next day. Word would get around and soon I'd find that I was the windlass expert. The next day I'd read up about battery charging. And so on…

These communities must be going on up and down the coasts all over the world. I'd noticed that the UK flags diminished quite quickly around the South Brittany coast. It was obviously the limit of a two week holiday from the UK. In Spain the UK registered boats were obvious cruising boats. In Povoa de Vazim there were several liveaboards; people who had sold up and now lived full time on boats. Often, these had made a conscious decision to leave the world of tax and regulation behind. They were invisible, despite the customs' interest, to the official world; modern hippies. I had to delete one photo because I'd inadvertently included one of them in it. There seemed to be a high proportion of ex-military in this contingent. I wondered if that's because they have the training to be self-sufficient and have had enough of authority. Others were professionals like Lee in La Coruna. They worked in this world taking people and boats around the world.

Gary and Sue were retirees. So was Ted. I always (presumably because of my nursing background) try to find out what people have retired from. Often the couples consist of the sailing man and the SWMBO (She who must be obeyed). The husband is being indulged for a few years until the grandchildren or great-grandchildren start to arrive. Then they will be tugged home by an invisible thread.

Others, like me, are late gap year travelers. Jonny and Sheila were maths teachers. They have sailed a twenty seven foot yacht around the Mediterranean before but are new to Atlantic sailing. They bought a thirty nine foot Dufour in Portugal a few weeks before. The night they launched it they invited a few of us around to celebrate. It was only nine foot longer than mine but it felt like a palace inside. They had low lighting all around, a fridge, two heads and enough space for six of us to laze around in comfort. We drank the red wine from the supermarket and the conversation wandered. It turned out that another couple, Dave and Marilyn, were from Grimsby. They had met John Beattie a couple of times. I was glad to hear this as I had heard no news of him since he wrote the suffix to his book in 1996. He was a gap year sailor too.

On Sunday Janet, Rob's girlfriend and fellow sailor, was joining me. Before she arrived there was a warning of a southerly gale. The problem is not the wind but the swell that travels up the gap between the breakwaters, swings around the harbour and then accelerates towards the pontoons. One of the long term boats last year had the gelcoat scraped off its bow. The marineros had moved all the yachts off one pontoon and refused entry to others arriving in the previous couple of days.

For the unattended boats they had produced lines of mooring rope and tied them in securely. They had asked us to double line secure and across from finger to finger of the pontoons. It looked like a regular cat's cradle.

I sat in my saloon planning the next few days. It was a Saturday and Janet was arriving the next day. I had learned not to underestimate Janet. She was another of AOAC's adventurous spirits. When I was learning to ski I had followed her down a hill, only for her to disappear way ahead of me. I once asked her for a dance in a salsa bar; she was excellent. When she was teaching me to paddle in white water I had found out that she had been a UK regional champion contender. She was joining me for the trip to Madeira. This was the first passage I'd be making since Biscay seven weeks ago; it felt a bit scary. The wind was in the South at Force 8. I had the North Atlantic chart; the ocean is very big and the islands are very small. We had to navigate our way across hundreds of miles of water to these tiny places, and we needed good weather to do it. A strong wind in the wrong direction was not good. The forecast showed a small window starting on Monday but the journey would take at least five days and probably seven. At that timescale the forecast begins to lose accuracy. And then during the day a remnant of an American hurricane began to show on the forecasts. It would hit Madeira a few days later with storm force winds. At the moment we would get there before the storm but that's like playing Russian roulette with the weather gods. It was no good: Janet's holiday finished on the next Monday; that put the lid on that passage for a while.

A big swell grew in the marina. The marineros were out every hour checking all the mooring lines. All of us were out checking them too. We had doubled the lines and retightened them over again. The pontoons were lifting over a metre up and down with the water. The boats tried to jerk themselves free against the lines. The spray over the breakwater was getting bigger and the sun was beginning to disappear in the warm, hazy wind.

I had a sense of waiting; waiting to see it out. All the fishing boats had moved into their inner harbour or down the coast. On the beach the fishermen were playing boules. From a distance it looked like they were slowly firing stones at each other. Their profile, silhouetted in the thin, misted sunshine, showed a throwing action, a short pause, and a spurt of earth would fly up like a mortar, near one of the others. They would crowd in to look, and another would throw. Another mortar would burst. Watching, it was like the watching a mystery. There was a hidden force waiting and we had to wait with it. We had to see what would happen. The air was thick behind them. The town front – a row of casinos with a wide promenade - was quietly vacant in the almost tangible, thickening air. It was slowly darkening, retreating into its own. It was a relief to go into a cafe. The telly was playing the VHF channel, top soundtracks to movies: Sliding Doors and Purple Rain. The videos were colourful reminders of our previous lives.

I met Alan and Sue outside. They were journeying slowly on their way to the Med. We promenaded through the town; a way of making the wait enjoyable. As we passed the fishing jetty Sue explained to me that the women sold fish from the backs of vans. A woman caught the word 'fish' and called us over. We were gently cajoled into buying some from the back of her van. We strolled on. Perhaps because of the waiting, the thick air, the sense of time closing down for the storm, we bought lottery tickets. It was a pointless idea. We would not be around to see the results. It just seemed to be a part of the waiting. They invited me to eat with them that night. I spent the evening enjoying their company in the comfort of their relative palace compared with my boat. I remembered what I'd written about the 'funny' stories of Portosin. It was good to realise that things were much better these days. I read them that passage, partly to explain how much I was enjoying the evening and, partly to remind myself. And then the rain started. I only had to run 200 metres to my boat but my underwear was wet through when I got back.

After a loud night of the rain hitting the decks I woke to go and meet Janet in Porto. She had planned to join me in Lisbon but I had asked her to meet me here instead. We travelled back on the metro in completely opposite conditions to when Hazel and I had ventured out not long before. It was pummeling rain against the windows. I felt guilty about inviting her to join me here in the rain when we were supposed to be in the sun, cruising to Madeira. We then had to negotiate the pontoons. By this time the sea swell from the wind had built to large waves, crashing over the breakwater. They formed breaking waves in the entrance to the harbour. The swell had managed to lift the pontoons up and down by over a metre. They flexed like octopus tendrils, the boats moved with them straining at their leashes. The squeak of fender against boat was amplified inside. Sleep was not easy that night. Three mooring lines broke and I lost another fender.

As the swell had diminished the next morning we went to look at the conditions outside. Walking along the breakwater involved dodging the spray that was still being sent up. All the other boat crews decided that it would be mad to leave. But we were both paddlers and could read the waves. Perhaps we were mad but we felt confident about leaving, so we went for it. We set off for Nazare 100 miles or so down the coast. Leaving the harbour was a bit like paddling off a beach to go kayak surfing. With the engine running fast we climbed up the front of five metre waves to go sliding down the back of them before climbing the next. Twenty minutes later we were far enough away to put the sails up. In light winds I went to the mast to hoist the sail. Although successful, I returned feeling more green than I have done for years. Janet was sitting in the cockpit looking just as bad. Within a few hours we had both been sick. That was the first time for me in thirty years.

We had not got far by midnight when the wind then changed to be on the nose. We had to tack down the coast for twenty eight hours. Deep joy. Maybe we could pull into a place that sounded remarkably like 'Finger of Fudge? (Foz de Figuera) The pilot book warns of breaking swell across the entrance. Too right: in the dark we rose on one swell and got my bearings for setting up the run in. As this pushed us a little off course we pulled back on the next swell. In the dark I could just see the previous swell rolling in and breaking as a great wave of surf across the whole width of the entrance. As I turned I heard Janet muttering that she didn't like the look of it. Neither did I. By the time she had finished the sentence I was heading fast back out to sea. We sailed on to Nazare; another twelve hours away. We got there almost exactly two days after setting out, tired, hungry, sick, and just glad to off the boat. But within ten hours we had walked into town twice, had a look around, supped the local coffee and eaten out in a Chinese restaurant. The next day we went up on a funicular railway, looked over the waves breaking on the headland and had a picnic lunch on the next beach. That was quite a difference.

Batilha (Battle Abbey) is a bit of Anglo-Portuguese history that had not made it into any book I had come across. A bus ride into the interior, it is a small town with an enormous abbey. The chap who built it did so to keep his end of the bargain when he prayed for victory over the Spanish. Having dispatched them he organised the building of this fantastically ornate abbey. It has the feel of York Minster about it. This is not surprising as he enlisted English architectural help. In fact this is yet another example of the two nations' cooperation over the centuries. The tomb inside has a statue of him and his English wife lying side by side and holding hands. The longest standing treaty in the world is between UK and Portugal; some hundreds of years old.

Apparently, this agreement was recognised again in 1982 when the Azores were provided as part of the supply chain to the Falklands War. The abbey had a feel of highly ornate cake decoration about it. It was all in white stone with the sort of carving I would expect on Lord Peter Wimsey chess pieces.

Although fascinating that's all there was to the town. After a warm up coffee we caught the bus back via another monastery town but I was monasteried out by then. Wet through we returned to the Safe Arrival to find that Ted had arrived from Povoa de Vazim on his boat, Edewsia. There was a note inviting us to eat with him that night. We couldn't refuse. It was Janet's last night before she returned to Lisbon. With a small hangover I saw her off at the bus station the next day and set about sorting me, the boat and provisions for a solo, six day passage to Madeira.

As she left I had a minor panic attack. Somehow it didn't seem possible that I could continue. I get this feeling whenever anyone leaves. Although, rationally, I know that the journey will go on and I will have good times there is something screaming at me that life will never be the same again. In my earlier years I would get very upset by this. Now I know that it is a feeling that will pass, although I still have to go through it.

I pottered about during the day with getting the boat ready. One annoying thing was that I needed diesel. Ted offered me some from his spare jerry cans so I topped up with that. I now know that my tank holds more than sixty litres as, with his and my cans, it was still not full. I had to go to the fuel pontoon anyway. That meant casting off, coming alongside and repeating this to get back to my pontoon ready to slip when the wind changed. The fuel pontoon was locked. I had to ring the bell, wait for them to open it, go up to the garage and prepay before filling up. But I didn't know exactly how much. I guessed, wrongly. I still owe Ted a few litres. When I got back to my berth he suggested rafting up to his boat so it would be easier to leave.

He was in conversation with a couple we had seen in a boat on the hard. They invited us back for nibbles. While we were there we discovered that they were from Chew Magna, near Bristol, and that their boat was one that Ted had worked on before they owned it. This is a small world. We talked Bristol and associated stuff. They invited us to stay for supper which was nice as I needed to eat and was in too much of a flurry to cook properly. With Ted having worked for Rolls Royce we all knew Bristol so a lot of memories were raised in a nostalgic night.

I went to bed early and set the alarm for every two hours. The wind was due to change and I wanted to catch every bit of it as it was only going to last for two days. Again I had broken the rule about sailing to timetables. I'd arranged to meet Anne Sofie in Madeira. I'd also arranged a time; that date was fast approaching. If I didn't leave now then I would probably miss her. She'd have to spend a week in Madeira on her own and without accommodation. I woke at midnight and immediately put the snooze on without actually looking out. Half an hour later I got a text from Hazel. It felt like a friendly reminder from England to get going. The wind had changed; after an hour of faffing about I slipped the lines and made for the harbour entrance.

On the way out I pulled in the fenders and lines and hoisted the sails. Out in the dark the harbour entrance looked very small. With the trepidation of up to six days on my own at sea it was easy to make anything look big enough a problem to turn back. As I turned out into the bay I set course over the swell. I orientated myself to the coast and turned the engine off. Off the coast there were two islands to miss before turning further south and crossing the shipping lanes. The islands had lighthouses on them but it was still a bit scary passing them.

Between the two there were a string of rocks and it was all too easy to see these as sticking out towards me in the dark. Even though I was sure that it was OK I still went back to the charts a few times to check. With only two hours sleep and it approaching daylight I was probably a bit more sensitive than usual. I thought back to the optical illusion when I was near Belle Isle and felt better.

At dawn I was past the islands. I would dearly have loved to sleep but I had twenty miles of shipping lane to cross. Off the coast of Portugal the lanes are divided into two going south and two going north. The outer ones are for ships carrying dangerous loads. I don't know why - any ship in these lanes was large enough to be lethal to me - but it sounded ominous: dangerous loads. It was the same as crossing the shipping lanes on the way to France except that I was travelling at forty five degrees to them so I spent longer crossing their paths. As the day progressed I got quite used to seeing them, time after time, alter course to miss me; but each time, until they did, it was still a worry that they may not have seen me.

Just after four o'clock I was clear and able to relax. I had a quick look about to check that there were no other vessels about and then went below for a sleep. I was so tired that first day that I could only think about tidying up and putting the mooring lines and fenders away. I actually did put them away the next day. The wind was a lovely Force 5 on a broad reach so we were creaming along. When I awoke a little while later it was in a hot flush. I didn't feel too good. To avoid cooking, I had one of Janet's ready meals. It was awful. I had to wash it down with a hot chocolate. At sunset I put in a reef just in case the wind got up during the night. I slept in short bursts rotating between sleep, tea, a piece of chocolate and back to bed. In the morning the sun came out; it was nice to be warm again after all those days of wind and rain. I started to clean up the mess of the day before.

I found that I got used to the solitude. I kept finding myself saying: "I've got five more days of this and that's OK. But how would I feel if it was another twenty nine?" I was thinking of the Atlantic crossing. In the afternoon I was overtaken by a catamaran a couple of miles away. I called them on the radio but no answer. I took a sun sight with the sextant. The rise of GPS has made this largely redundant but I learnt how to do this in case my electrical systems all went down. As I don't need to know my position more accurately than to find a large island it is relatively easy. I remember my brother telling me about the paradigm shift in thinking that led to the means of establishing an accurate position. For centuries sailors had been trying to work out where they were. But some clever thinking worked out that this was the wrong way around. If you say "I think I'm here," as an educated guess, and take a reading of the sun it will show you that you are wrong. I can then work out how far I am wrong. I plot that against my guess and it tells me where I am. On this first practise at sea I wasn't too far out. I also set up my short wave radio to receive the weather fax.

I made half way during the night but the wind slowly died. I knew this was going to happen and that it would come against me by the end of the day. I motored to get as far south as I could before then. The morning emerged, flat, sunny and glassy calm. The time slid by. I would sit and think for a few minutes and two hours had gone by. The sea was beginning to form into long swells, big valleys. When I saw a ship in the distance I would look through the binoculars to check its course. When it disappeared behind a wave it would appear that a great wall of water was coming at me. I had to look above the binos to check that it was just an ordinary wave several times until I got used to it. The wind was teasing. With the engine on it sometimes appeared to be strong enough to sail but it took several hours before I could stop the engine. And then, as predicted, I was close hauled but still on course.

The next days were a bit of a blur. I had no fixed moments, no fixed routine to keep to. I tried to fill in the log every two hours but it was sometimes several hours between entries. Close hauled it was not a nice movement. The boat jumped about a bit and I lost the inclination for everyday domestics. I forced myself to cook and clean up but it was in short bursts. It was too bumpy to read. I was in the middle of a book about a man hitchhiking his way around Scotland by boat. I knew a lot of the places he was visiting. It seemed strange to be in the vast emptiness of the ocean and reading about sailing in Scotland. And then the showers set in and it was too wet to read.

Out at sea you get clued in to the clouds. They usually mean something. But, on the weatherfax, there was "trough" close by. That was beyond my understanding. The clouds were at all levels and just about all types. There were big swathes of 'baguettes' just like the trails from jets at high altitude. These are supposed to indicate deteriorating weather but they were disintegrating just like vapour trails. There were hundreds of little cotton wool things at low level. They appeared by day but were gone by night. In between there were marauding grey glooms that would sweep across the horizon to seek me out. I'm sure they were intelligent in the way that they would find me. The rain would begin to patter and then the wind would whoosh to set the drops to sting force. I'm glad I had a roller-reefing genoa. I'm beginning to think differently about in-mast reefing too. Except when it jams, it is much easier to reef. I've been to the mast so many times to reef while the boat rolls on the waves that the thought of being able to stay in the cockpit seems pure luxury. I'm beginning to think that I would like to sail a catamaran too. They don't roll about nearly as much and they are faster. Maybe next time I do this journey? I found that she likes me reefing the main first. That way I can adjust by rolling the genoa in. And she sails well with the storm jib up all the time as a cutter rig. At night I took in a bit more sail to reduce the chances of having to go up on deck in the dark.

I returned to the thought of sailing the Atlantic solo several times. The pattern seemed to be that, once at sea, it's the same. Even half way had been just that; a marker. There was still more of the same to go. But as I got closer to the end I became impatient. The 100 miles to go point was frustrating. In my previous life, on land, 100 miles is about a two hour drive; now it was twenty four hours. Perhaps it was a mixture of anxiety over pilotage and mooring in an unknown port combined with a yearning for shore life luxuries. Once I was there I would be able to have showers, coffee, beer and wi-fi. It's easy to do without these things but once the idea returned then I wanted them right now. It was difficult to realise that this was for tomorrow at the earliest. If I had been on the Atlantic crossing then I would have another twenty days to go. Would this feeling wait until the last day or would it visit me on other occasions? I have remembered similar feelings on holidays before. I'm quite happy wandering around and would quite happily extend my time away if something came up. However, on the last day I wake up wanting just to get home. Anything that is not focused on that is an irritation, irrelevant.

I also thought of all the people I'd met so far. The crowd from Povoa de Vazim near Porto were the strongest community I'd been in. Unfortunately, most of them were heading towards the Algarve or Mediterranean. I'd particularly miss Ted. I'd first heard of him in Gijon and then a couple of other places until I caught up with him in Baiona. Another solo sailor we had sort of joined forces in our journeys. He had built his own steel boat from scratch and his knowledge of sailing was incredible. I had first heard him as he passed my boat on the jetty: "That's a Bowman Rival 32 with an Aries wind vane. A super little boat." He'd pointed out that my wind generator blades were back to front and helped me reset them. For this he'd provided the sprocket puller. He'd then changed the bearings on his. Was there anything he didn't have aboard? One thing was an aerial for his wi-fi. He'd bought and paid for one on the internet with Jim, off Ocean Warrior, when he was in Baiona. It was slowly catching up with him as he travelled down the coast of Portugal. It had got to him, via three other boats, shortly before I left. When we'd walked into town one day I found that he had an even more Velcro mind than I have. We never made more than about fifty metres through the boatyard without him stopping to exclaim about a yacht. He knew ninety percent of the designs and thought about the modifications on them. I could see the ideas being processed as he wondered if he could use them himself. And I learnt so much from him: electrics, food storage, sailing strategy, carpentry, wind vanes. Just in general conversation I gleaned so much useful stuff about my journey.

Porto Santo is a favourite stopping over point for yachts in transit. I arrived at 05.30, possibly the worst time to arrive. I had used up all the night and had none left to sleep in. From midnight I had been waking every twenty minutes to look out for fishing boats and other shipping. I raised a lighthouse from twenty miles out. I had spent twenty minutes working out which way a ship was going until I realised its lights were really street lights on a hill. As I rounded the eastern end I again got confused by the lights. It looked like there was a giant contraption in the bay. Slowly it dawned on me that this was the street lights on another hill combined with a housing estate. I found my way into the harbour and made a recce. There were plenty of spaces so I rigged the lines and fenders and slid onto a finger pontoon. It had taken me five days and five hours to travel 520 miles. Suddenly I realised what I had just done. I didn't know whether to laugh or cry, shout or scream. I didn't do any. I put the alarm on and went to sleep.

I woke to a brilliant sun. I'd not felt this heat before, not even in Spain; and certainly not for the last two weeks. I pulled myself out of a deep slumber to go and get the customs and marina formalities out of the way. When I spoke to Anne Sophie on the phone she told me that she was coming on the ferry the next day. It was sensible thinking as, if I had not arrived that day, she would have had to find somewhere to stay and Porto Santo is expensive. It has the only natural beach in the Madeira archipelago so it is a favourite holiday resort amongst the rich Madeirans. It also gave me time to recover and clean up. But I was slightly sorry as I was set up in my mind for conversation. Everything I've heard in the last few days I've already known as I was the one who said it. I had tried to listen to Wild Swans on a talking book; but that is not a jolly story.

The harbour wall is, like many transit ports on the North Atlantic, painted by the crews of passing yachts. Each one is different with the name of the yacht, sometimes the crew, and the date. Some are artistic while some are straightforward lists. I wondered if Safe Arrival was there although I don't think that she has been beyond the Azores before. If she had it would have been earlier than 1984. The wall looked younger than that. The shower block was basic but clean. I showered and shaved, found the bar, sat down to my first coffee and am now checking my emails. Life is back to normal.

7 ISLAND LIFE: THE START

While sitting, taking in my new surrounding, in the bar at Porto Santo harbour, I noticed an older couple arrive. They sat at a table near me. They were obviously English and retired; they greeted the waiter with warm recognition. After a while I struck up a conversation with them. They had first come here in 1986. Then, they had stayed a week. Over the years they had come back again and again, first for weeks and then, when they had retired, for months at a time. When I told them that I was a yottie they recoiled at first. It seems that they have been avid sailing blog readers. They are upset by the poor press given to this island. I could see what they meant. Although it is definitely a resort island it has a charm to it. I've no idea what it would have been like in high season but, at that moment, it was quiet with a small community feeling. They told me where the shops were and recommended I stayed in the bar for lunch.

Later, while I was checking up on maintenance things, I met a family from Swansea. I had been to Swansea earlier in the year when taking Safe Arrival for sea trials in the Bristol Channel. I invited them for sundowners that evening but they countered with an offer for supper. They had caught tuna the day before on the way across; it needed eating. We exchanged notes about the passage with them having been a few hours ahead of me. The tuna was lovely. The son taught me about lures and lines. He then modified one of theirs as a gift to me. Sometimes on this trip I have been embarrassed by people's generosity. I have nothing to repay it besides my company and some malt whisky. I can fit two or three more in my cockpit but it is uncomfortable compared with the modern yacht palaces. I don't feel beholden like a poor country cousin; we come from all backgrounds. It is generally quite recognised that some of us were going small, going cheap and going now. It is the community of the travelling sea folk. What moves people to help me or make gifts? Perhaps, in another life, I would be able to repay my debts.

I had intended to have an early night that night but we sat there nattering until late. I got up the next morning, early enough to potter about making the boat presentable but not late enough for my tired head. Anne Sophie arrived on the ferry. It was good to see a familiar face although she was trailing an enormous bag behind her. Would it fit on the boat I wondered? We spent the afternoon walking along the beach; right from one end back, all seven kilometres, to the marina. I vaguely remember that the conversation ranged around relationships, weather and home making. The next day we set sail for Madeira. Anne Sophie had made a list of all the marinas, levadas and bus routes. We decided to go into Quinta do Lorde, a small marina at the eastern end and walk levadas near there. I was to realise that, in Madeira, to misquote Eisenhower: "Our plan is nothing, our planning is nothing either!"

Quinta do Lorde is a purpose built resort. The marina hides below a high cliff that looks like a large landslide left it behind. The dramatic face, in golden brown, is topped by a small hut. Below, the yachts huddle for safety at the base protected by the marina; a line of angled bank, stones and concrete, a small road and a line of low buildings set in a small crescent surround the yachts. At the end, where the breakwater meets the marina, is a small bar like any marina bar around the world. There is a programme about sailing on the TV. Above it, though, is a small house with a modern lighthouse extending off the roof. There is no practical reason for the lighthouse, no historical need. It is a feature, a folly, a designer's romantic notion realised for this isolated toytown resort.

Our plan was to catch a bus to a walk a levada but we discovered that the busses don't run connecting services and we would need to change. That meant that we could not get there and back in the same day. We couldn't afford a taxi so that was that. Instead we walked to the east end of the island. Within minutes of leaving the marina we were in a new land; more of an old land really as it becomes clear that this Madeira is an old volcano. The magma colours with basalt form shapes that could have been the influence for Gormanghast. We walked up and down the cliffs to the end of the island where the visitors' centre, staffed by a man who walks there each day, provides nothing but benches. It was an old bothy-type hut which now has a few rooms to hire but nothing else. We sat on the bench eating our packed lunch and feeding the lizards. They were very tame; they came up on the table and ate off my hand not, initially, by design. I had my hand relaxed on the table when I felt something touch it. A bit shocked we noticed that they had a passion for apple. As soon as I bit into mine they all started looking up. One even followed my hand about. Sophie put her core down on the little stone wall where they seemed to queue to fight over it. Between them they could move it a fair distance. Little creatures, about ten centimetres, they were fantastically alert and could move around at speed. I could see where Spielberg got his ideas for Jurassic Park from. I fell asleep with my head on the table and Anne Sophie took pictures of one of them coming to visit the crumbs of bread right by me.

In the evening we decided to eat aboard. Although I had budgeted for eating out once a week, the bar menu was too disappointingly English, not worth it. The next morning we visited another Rival. On the way in the owner had hailed us. I wasn't sure if I recognised him but I certainly recognised the bow of his boat. Pam and Bruce showed us around; it had some similarities to my boat but was so well kept and spacious that, from inside, you wouldn't have known that it was a variation on mine. The only clue was that the bulkhead (the internal wall between the saloon and the galley/chart desk) had the trademark keyhole, or phallic shape, passageway cut into it. Bruce and Pam, the owners, had been travelling for a couple of years. They had 'done' the Mediterranean and were now about to do the Caribbean. At that point they were recovering from having got caught in the gale that Janet and I had avoided. Later, in the bar, I was approached by my first Atlantic hitchhiker. Lena, a sturdy Swede, and her absent boyfriend were a bit fed up with travelling on a French yacht and she was tipsy enough to say so.

As Anne Sophie had already spent three days in Funchal we decided that Calheta would be a good place to approach the westerly levadas from. The central ones were closed owing to really bad floods the previous February and, still burning, fires from August. In my haste to leave Quinta I didn't check that the coast was clear sufficiently. The day before we had seen a three-masted square rigger anchor outside the harbour. It never occurred to me to check whether this large vessel was actually coming into the marina. One of the beauties of my boat is the longish keel. It means that it goes in a straight line at sea. The downside is that it is a pig to manoeuvre in tight spaces, especially going backwards. I had to back off from this monster and keep control with little blips on the throttle for ten minutes while the marina ribs nudged the large ship onto a pontoon like tugs to a tanker. Eventually, once my stress levels were up to yachtmaster exam level, there was enough room to exit. We set sail for a six hour motor to Calheta.

Calheta was another toytown marina under a cliff. It did have three places to eat and drink though. One was run by a South African, one by a Dutchman and the other looked to be run by Germans. It also had a hotel and a supermarket. We enquired about busses; there was one in the morning and one in the evening. People were surprised when we wanted to walk into town. We found out why; there is no centre to it but a straggling residential mass, dotted with the odd shop. The houses look like they may be sliding over the edge of the cliff. The marina was the only semblance of a centre. We also found that the busses weren't going to get us to and from any levadas from here either. At least we could have a nice meal and plan how to get to some levadas by going back to Funchal the next day. But already the weather was plotting against us. The few drops of rain that evening turned, by degrees, to thundering rain by the next morning. We slept in, waiting for it to abate. The trickles down the cliff the night before had turned to thundering waterfall like when a mains pipe bursts on a hilly street; only these were vertical. By midday the marina water was brown and full of vegetation washed off the hills. When I flushed the heads the bowl was left with muddy water in it. Funchal was flooded with half a metre of water in the streets and the rivers bursting their banks. The marina was not accepting visitors. We stayed another night in toytown.

We ate out again. Anne Sophie got talking to another couple as we sat down so we joined them. Lu was Cuban married to Jean Michel. Unusually, in my experience, for a Frenchman, he had a good command of several languages. As Anne Sophie speaks both their languages and I can understand a bit the conversation was mainly in French and Spanish. Occasionally they had to break into English for me. The hardest bit was that they kept changing half-way through a sentence. Jean Michel was a very experienced sailor and knew how to get around all the rules. He gave me plenty of tips for travelling. He had a habit of finishing off a sentence with a short 'pff' as if he was imitating a bicycle tyre valve being released. With this he would hang his head forward over his chest and make his mouth into an 'O' shape as if to make blow a smoke ring. Despite that he smoked heavily he didn't blow any rings.

Before we left for Funchal the next morning we went for coffee and to look around their boat. It was a Westerly Centaur, one of the types I had considered but found too expensive. I liked the stern cabin behind a centre cockpit. He had bought it cheap in Spain and was doing it up. I didn't envy him this at all.

It had been used as a floating, static caravan. It was in good domestic state but the sailing and engine states were in dire need of attention. Too much for me I thought.

We got to Funchal only to find that all the possible levadas would be in a dangerous condition from the rain the day before. So we went for a walk along the promenade. At a stop for coffee a couple at another table seemed to get under Anne Sophie's skin. She found them more and more annoying. When she got up to fill her bottle from a water fountain it whooshed high in the air and splashed them. They appeared coldly irritated. Muttering something about senses of humour Anne Sophie seemed to get even more annoyed. I half expected her to blame them for her lack of levada walking but we continued with our walk soon after. It was a bit overwhelming to be back in crowds after so long. It was hot and there were plenty of Brits about. I felt out of place.

I met another old memory. Ten years before I had been repatriating a patient from Funchal when the engineer, whose job it was to tick the box stating that the airplane stretcher was OK, had not appeared. Consequently, my patient could not travel on the plane. We had a twenty four hour delay in the Funchal Savoy courtesy of British Airways. And here I was outside the Savoy again. Suddenly lots of geography settled into place. In the time between, the marina had been created in the harbour. I remembered watching crowds of people queuing to catch the ferry to an island during a public holiday. Could they have been off to Porto Santo? There was no marina then, it was just a harbour. Now the steps they had queued down led onto a pontoon with lots of stationary boats moored against it. I also remembered being refused service in one of the Savoy restaurants because I was wearing fluorescent orange shorts. I didn't mind as I went downtown and had a superb sardine meal in a bar where I watched it all being cooked in the front. I did, however, go back stinking of sardines.

We went searching for some evening life but it all seemed quiet. We had a beer in the theatre cafe sitting watching what seems to be the gay meeting point. On the way back we found that the night life was all just by the boat; we had been sitting on top of it all the time. There was a salsa band playing in a bar. We watched for a while and went back to the boat. After a bit I decided to go back. I got dressed in suitable clothes and went into the bar to buy a drink. As I got outside to dance they changed their style; they only played a local dance from then on. I sat drinking my beer and observing; there was a definite set of dynamics. There were youngish couples who only danced with each other. There were older couples who only danced with each other. Then there were one or two blokes who could dance better than the rest who asked several women to dance. There were lots of young women who danced in lines, arm in arm, with their other women friends and organised little routines between themselves. Lastly, there were the grandmothers. Their role seemed to be to make sure that their granddaughter was plainly dressed, had no make up; and to prevent her from dancing. This supervision seemed so unfair; let them see paradise but deny it to them.

We spent the next morning sorting through bus timetables, levada maps and getting increasingly irritated that we couldn't square the two. Then we missed a bus. By now we were laughing at Anne Sophie's levada jinx. And then she found one. We hopped on a bus and got put off at the wrong point. Luckily, it was only a short walk to get to the start of the walk. At last Anne Sophie got her levada. Despite that it was raining in bursts and that the bank was muddy and that, in a 300 metre tunnel, we paddled through twenty centimetre puddles, we enjoyed it. It was a bit like narrow boat cruising but the canal was only a metre wide and we had no boat. Every now and then there was evidence of the floods. Landslips and bare patches of earth showed where the sheer weight of the water had overpowered the normal drainage and carried it all away.

Back at the boat we had showers and then I saw Anne Sophie to the bus stop. Just as it arrived the Swansea family walked past and started conversation. At the same time the people Anne Sophie had met on the way out greeted her on to the bus. In what seemed like an instant, we had gone from standing at the side of the road to our separate ways. It was the most instant goodbye I think I had ever experienced. I had a beer with the family before they caught the bus back to their toytown marina. Then I went back to the boat to contemplate my plans.

With Anne Sophie gone I had eleven days until James arrived. He had been delayed by work but that meant I had more time to get a few things sorted. I still seemed to be carrying the tiredness from the crossing to Porto Santo. I was mildly concerned by this as I began to wonder what that would mean for a thirty day crossing. Inspired by Sophie's love for fruit I went to the Fruit Market. It looked like many of the ones I'd happily wandered about over the previous months. However, I was set upon by some very friendly fruiterers who plied me with all sorts of delicious fruit. Despite insisting that I only had only bought a few pieces before making my retreat to the street, I realised I had been stung. I must remember not to go to the market when tired.

Despite having a list of things to do I couldn't raise any enthusiasm for them. I spent my time wandering, soaking up the feeling of Funchal, and reading. I read three books in a week. Only very slowly did I start to get the boat sorted. I seemed to be thinking this through concrete: what food would I need for the crossing, where to go in the canaries; what questions to ask my contacts in Grenada. Was I really at the point where I was finding out about the customs house in Prickly Bay?

Slowly it dawned on me, in my planning, that I had a cold. It had never occurred to me that I could get a trifling illness like that. I had sorted out a medicine box for serious problems like infections and breakages; but a cold? Anyway, once I gave into the sore throat and blocked ears I set into a pattern for a couple of days. I spent my time between reading, coffee in cafes and checking the cruise liners in and out. There are so many of them. The first day we arrived there was an enormous one that had stayed a few days. It was only after it left and its space was taken by three others that I realised quite how big it was. Oriana's sister ship the Oceana appeared one day. They stay such short times. There is hardly time for the passengers to get ashore before they are being herded back on and off to the next port. My type of cruising seems to be boat maintenance in different ports while their cruising seems to be sheep imitation in different ports.

I enjoyed watching the harbour pilots in action. They would bring these enormous cruise ships out backwards, twist in confined spaces and turn out for the ocean. As they did so a little craft would hang alongside, take the pilot off and shoot back to the port. Anne Sophie had earlier observed that I seemed to like activities that involved twisting and turning. I thought about that: dancing, sailing, paddling, skydiving and skiing all involve them. And then I wondered if that wasn't the nature of life. We get all sorts of things thrown at us and we manoeuvre as best we can to make the best of our circumstances. Are these other activities that we take up used to satisfy the risk appetite that is left hungry by a perceived safe life at home?

If my philosophical ponderings were correct the guy playing the panpipes above the harbour was running on far too easy a ride. Having listened to his repertoire (My Way, Don't cry Argentina, Simon and Garfunkel, Robbie Williams, Abba,) repeated at least four times a day for a week, he was in potential danger of being escorted into the sea; and deep sea at that. Well that's the way I felt; the insidious easy listening of it was driving me mad. The constant and unavoidable sound intruded just about everything I did. Perhaps this was because I was mainly in my own thoughts for a week. With my hardly leaving the boat and snoozing the cold off I didn't have many conversations. I felt a bit lonely in the city; the mass of tourists made me invisible. I was used to the camaraderie of the sailing community. Madeira is a tourist island and I found it hard to find a comfortable place ashore. I asked a barman in one place if anyone made an effort to speak Portuguese. He couldn't think of many instances; he added that his income depended on them so he "followed the tourists" and spoke English.

On the first morning of feeling better I was struck by an apparition. A young, obviously English, woman was walking along the pontoon bridge. She had just got out of an unusual tender that I recognised as belonging to Rusty, a yacht anchored just outside. She was wearing a bright red summer dress and walking with that jaunty style that Julie Christy had in the beginning of Billy Liar. After a short conversation she, Charlotte, rowed off to her boat. But that evening I came across her again with the rest of her crew in a harbourside bar. Charlotte had been on her own boat, until the Algarve, with her partner and their five year old, Jake. There she had joined up with Rusty's crew. The five of them were a young and very comfortable crowd. I stayed all night with them, quite forgetting all my washing out to dry and the pile of maintenance that I had at last got around to sorting. Jake was a lucky kid; practically born in a boat he now had his mum and three other big kids to play with all the time. He seemed totally unfazed by the attention of adults and not spoilt at all. And here he was about to cross the Atlantic at the age of five, nearly fifty years younger than me.

We stayed in the bar until the music outside was too much

to ignore; we went to investigate. There were two men in suits, one singing and the other playing a keyboard computer. They were so bad that they were almost good. We danced the night away, almost salsaing to the awful music. Later, when we were all tired and drunk I had a go in Rot, Rusty's tender. She was a homemade design of James, the skipper; two halves of a sharp canoe bolted together midships. She was very tippy and I nearly went in trying to get in. Then I remembered my balance and relaxed. That worked well for a few seconds until I tried to put the oar in a rowlock. I was nearly over again. I successfully rowed around for a few minutes acutely conscious of my drunken state, the probable temperature of the water and my poor swimming skills. Then I watched them all pile in, settle themselves down and row off out of the harbour to their boat. I was invited to Halloween onboard the next evening. Best think out an outfit.

The Halloween was not up to the same standard, perhaps because we had been out the night before; we were all a bit tired. However, we had an enjoyable, relaxed time except, notably, for the ride there. With all six of us in her Rot was stable and cut a fine line through the water. Until, that is, we got into the sea outside the harbour. There the wave length was just right for tipping one end in to collect water while it lifted the other out. Jake was getting worried and I was silently panicking behind the oarsman. All those comments about the most accidents happening in the tender were mixed up with my lack of lifejacket. Fortunately, there was a large catamaran moored nearby. We discharged three people while James rowed the rest of us to Rusty and collected them later. By the time I was rowed home the waves were a bit smaller; Rot loved it sliding down the fronts of these little rollers. In the front, lying and looking backwards I could see the rest of the boat lift up and then feel the acceleration as we plunged towards the next wave and lifted over it. It was as if I had switched off the fear factor from the outward journey and let the exhilaration free. Or maybe it was that I was nearer home and could relax.

I bumped into Rusty's crew several more times over the next few days. I was lucky with meeting them I thought. They were an eclectic crowd with an enormous and complimentary set of skills. Between them they could cook, build boats, sail, paint, row, entertain and teach Jake while also having skills in photography, computers, electrics and various other things. What I also liked was that they kept up an inventive banter. The heads became 'the room of epiphany' when one of them kept emerging saying "I've just had a thought..." They were on an express passage, in yachting terms, to Antigua but I hoped to catch up with them there.

James, Janet's brother, arrived and we set up for the journey to Graciosa, just north of Lanzarote. I'd spent nearly three weeks in Madeira and, although keen to get moving, I felt as if I was pulling up the tiny beginnings of roots.

During the last few days in Funchal the swell had slowly been getting worse. Rusty came in from anchoring outside to lie alongside the harbour wall, as did a couple of other boats. One of them I realised was the Norwegian boat that Hazel had got chatting with in Baiona. The skipper had a new crew for the ARC; a couple unknown to him had contacted via web links and were now about to sail the Atlantic with him. The ARC is the Atlantic Rally for Cruisers It provides the routing and practicalities, not to mention the paperwork, for crews not sure about an Atlantic crossing. It also provides camaraderie in the form of a big party in Las Palmas and another in Rodney Bay, St Lucia. They leave in late November so they can be there for Xmas. Those of us who can't afford it profess disdain and go later when the trade winds are more settled. At one time there was a club called NARC whose sole purpose was not to be the ARC. The names painted on the harbour wall are testament to the number of boats that have participated in its twenty five year history.

As the swell increased it became more uncomfortable in the harbour too so I was not unhappy to be leaving. We got ourselves sorted and left just after lunch on the Thursday. Being a high, volcanic island the wind swerves around Madeira. We were in strong gusting winds as we left the harbour. I put in reefs and we raised six knots. Like this we would make a short journey. Of course, as we moved away from the land the wind dropped; I shook out all the reefs as James retired below to ward off sea sickness. Our course for Lanzarote would have been a close haul but, as the wind was due to swing north on Saturday, I set a close reach. Although this increased our journey distance slightly it gave more speed and, more importantly, less uncomfortable motion. It didn't help James though; he was sick. I made a chicken casserole for supper that night but he gave it back to the sea not long after.

We took it in turns to wake up and look around that night. It's a form of watch keeping: one sleeps while the other dozes and pops their head out every now and then. There are so few ships out here that the chances of coming upon one are very slight. When we did go up and look about the sight of the stars held us there for ages. They were so bright. There was no moon; the background was inky black. It was difficult to make out the constellations because there were so many other stars within them; these are the stars we don't normally see in the cities. Orion has an aura, a powerful warrior look about him. I'm still trying to get used to the plough being below the horizon.

On Friday very little changed: James was still sea sick, two French yachts that left at the same time as us had long since disappeared in the night. I began to wonder what the difference between solo sailing and having a crew was. I spent most of it on my own and in my own thoughts. I was beginning to recognise the pattern of passage making. I had the same physical feelings as before, the sense of being in the middle of nowhere, the loss of time scale, the rolling of the boat were all the same as before. I didn't feel like doing much. I ate comfort food. The big difference was that James would emerge every now and then. I dozed off and on too.

Gradually the wind shifted and we began to make a better course. Overnight we got to head in the right direction but in the morning the wind died. We got the motor running. Both of us felt much better; refreshed. We both started to cook properly, clean up and generally begin to actively embrace the journey. I took a navigation sunsight, made some awful mistakes in my calculations but eventually, after the second one, I estimated us to be within five miles of the GPS plot. We got out the fishing gear and, after some discussion, set up a lure about twenty metres behind the boat. It was a bit of a shock to find that we had a bite within minutes. As I pulled in we could see a yellow fin tuna jumping and thrashing behind us. We were so excited. I've never fished before and now we had a vision of supper. I stupidly tried to pull in the line without gloves and burnt my fingers as the tuna pulled back. James got ready to haul it in. As neither of us had any experience of getting hold of a fifty centimetre flapping fish we weren't really sure of what to do. However, just as we lifted it clear of the water it got away. The knot we'd tied to the lure had come undone. Supper was gone; and so was our lure. This had been specially prepared for me by the Swansea family. We tried with another lure but nothing else came our way. That night we ate risotto.

In the night, sailing again, the lights of Lanzarote glowed over the horizon. By dawn we could see one of its northern islands. Slowly, we made our way around and between the islands to a narrow passage between Lanzarote and Graciosa. In the hot, midday sun the wind died again so we motored the last couple of miles into what appeared to be a frontier town harbour. We were scanning the moorings for a free space when we heard loud whistles. Two uniformed men were signaling to us to go over. They looked almost paramilitary. They had assumed the job of organising the harbour on the weekend when Pedro, the marinero, was not there. His was very much a one man marina.

Ashore for the first time in three days we went to find a cafe, had coffee, beer and tortilla before returning to put the boat to bed. On the way back we met a German couple, Max and Gude, who were sailing the circuit on a tiny Folkboat. It was so small that they didn't have a guardrail. They had tried to join the ARC but their boat was too short. Max told us that he had written to the organisers but that they had replied explaining that there was a minimum length for a reason. Max understood English humour very well. He said he didn't know the English could say "F*** off" so nicely! He seemed to have been reared on a diet of Black Adder; he called us Tommies, did a bad German accent very well and had all the nuance of intonation to keep both us two Brits and the two other Germans we met laughing all evening.

To get an idea of Graciosa you have to imagine a narrow stretch of water, sided to the south by a cliff, and, to the north, an island, itself a long sandy beach with yachts anchored off. At the end of the beach is a small harbour with a few ferry boats going in and out plus an occasional yacht. The only village fronts on to the harbour. There are lines of white, two-storey houses lined up for a few hundred metres. In between the Land Rovers parked on the sand roads give the feeling of a desert training camp for soldiers posted to Iraq. And yet the white-washed, architect-designed houses are cared for with flowers and tiled walls. Behind the houses the volcanic, barren rock rises to a couple of peaks. It looks like a dollop of lava was dropped there like a dropped, melted ice cream. There is nothing more. There is a complete lack of any sense of time. We managed to spend a whole day doing nothing more than drinking a few coffees, a few beers and going for a walk.

Unfortunately, a storm, way to the north, was predicted to send a five metre swell down to us. Reluctantly we made our way down to Arricife, the capital of Lanzarote. There were two harbours there; one is industrial while the old fishing one has, apart from the fishing school, become more of an anchorage for travelling yachts; and some that have obviously not travelled for years. On our first evening the anchor dragged so we said 'hello' to Macy, an American, wooden boat, at closer quarters than we envisaged. They were very nice about it; the same thing had happened to them a few nights before.

We spent a couple of days mooching around the town before James flew home. After he left I needed to get some things sorted out. In exploring further I discovered an IKEA. As I was tired after a long and dusty walk to the oil refinery, only to find out that they don't refill my type of gas cylinder, I wandered in. IKEA didn't feel like home but it was a strangely comfortable experience. Unfortunately I lost my sunglasses in there.

I needed water. This was the first time that I had not had a hose pipe close by. It was time to try out an idea I got from a yacht in Spain. I had adapted my old flexible water tank, the one that died in Baiona, to fit in the dinghy. I rowed it down to a tap and filled it up. Having a poor connection it started filling the dinghy too. I rowed back up wind with my feet in four inches of water. The second problem was that the hose I had planned to pump the water out of the tank and into the boat was stored in a flat roll. And it stayed flat despite me trying to pump water through it. My hosepipe fitted too loosely to leave it alone so I had to sit for twenty minutes in a flooded dinghy holding the pipe to the pump while the sun went down, and the temperature with it. At least I had water for when Bridge and Michala arrived the next day.

8 ISLAND LIFE CONTINUED

Time gets confusing when journeying. Apart from the lack of routine to my days it was the sun that confused me. There are four factors to the length of the day. Firstly, the further West I went the later the sun rises and the later it sets. I think that Bristol is eight minutes behind London. Then there are the seasons; the longer days in summer and shorter in winter. Then add in latitude: Kenya, on the equator, hardly moves from a twelve hour day whatever season. Finland gets nearly twenty four hour days in summer and hardly any day light in winter. Just in case that's not enough then there is the time zone that the country chooses to be in. Portugal, west of France and most of Spain, chooses to keep in the same time zone as UK. As Madeira is part of Portugal it keeps with it despite being way west. However, having travelled from Madeira to Lanzarote, arguably part of Spain, one week after daylight saving time returned to GMT I expected to return to GMT plus one. Consequently, I arrived at the airport to meet Bridge and Michala at what I thought was twenty minutes before their flight. I should have twigged that something was amiss as the bus stop seemed to be giving inappropriate information. Somewhere, my calculations had gone wrong. I finally welcomed them to Lanzarote nearly two hours after arriving at the airport.

We started the way that we carried on for most of the week: we had a couple of beers in town. Then, after shopping and settling in to the boat, we invited the American boat, Macy, next to us for gin and tonics. As they already had supper on the go we went to visit them. They had built their boat from the hull themselves. It was wooden. All the lovely crafting was their work. Between them they had taken ten years to finish it and had been sailing for three years. They were on the way home after a circumnavigation. They would soon be making for Grenada where Macy would be coming out, again, for painting. I wondered if I'd see them there. Slightly tipsy, we rowed ashore and had a superb meal in a tapas bodega that Michala found. I keep forgetting that it's not summer in the UK but they reminded me that they'd got up in the freezing cold, and had been travelling since four in the morning, and then they fell asleep quite early.

The next day we motored north back to Graciosa, against the wind and current, to anchor in the dark. It took us several attempts to lay an anchor that wouldn't drag and even then we weren't sure about it. I set the GPS alarm and we went to bed only to be woken by it a couple of hours later. Sleep is very difficult when you know that there is a reef only 200 metres away and my year is over if the boat hits it. As the wind was rising the waves got big enough to snatch at the chain. If it could take this snatching then it was now firmly set. I had to put out a snubber to stop the snatch. At last we could sleep.

The idea was to go swimming before breakfast but the morning was windy and grey. So a quick dip was all we could manage. It was like an English summer's day so we expected the water to be bracing at least. Actually, it was quite warm. But it was not comfortable at anchor so we made our way into the marina. It was becoming apparent that Michala was not suffering from sea sickness but had some ailment. She had been pumped full of injections the week before ready for a trip to Africa so maybe they were upsetting her systems. We chilled with coffee and beers for the rest of the day while enjoying the quiet life of Graciosa. The next day was just as chilled; a long walk around the coast to climb a bit of a volcanic hill. On the way we watched the surfers. They were obviously good but the waves were breaking only shortly before a reef so they had only about five seconds to stand up before breaking off them. While we were there some body-boarders joined them. Now they had fun. They were on the waves as they formed to break right or left and get 'in the tube.' I've never seen that before except on the adverts. To see it in real life was breathtaking.

The hill behind was covered in different forms of erosion. The waves had cut out smooth grooves from the base while the wind had blown off the lava crusts from one side. The sandstone, which we thought must be sea bed raised by the volcano, was soft and broke into sand at a touch. There were little gullies formed by rain. All this combined to produce a collage of different reds and yellows with black coating. On the way back we investigated all the rock pools for life. I am always surprised by differing things that people see. While I can look at the sky and make a weather assessment or spot yacht and aircraft manoeuvres I can also be totally unaware of the wildlife or flora within feet of me. Michala could see signs of octopus. She spotted various fish and named them. Each of the pools had different characteristics and she would change her way of seeing with them. Back in Baiona, Hazel had asked me how I knew so much about sailing and all the stuff that goes with yachts. I supposed that it was that I had been around them for so long. I realised that this was true for Michala; she had been involved in water and diving for some years, at times professionally. In that time she had absorbed a lot of working knowledge. Later in the week she spotted a Kestrel on a balcony.

During my longer passages I had been troubled by my power management. The batteries on Safe Arrival seemed to last for two days before they needed more recharging than the wind generator and the solar panel could supply. The biggest user of power, on passages, is the tri-colour navigation light at the top of the mast. In Funchal, Rusty had suggested that I bought an LED light as they use about an eighth of the power. Bridge had brought one out from England and it was time to fit it. That meant climbing to the top of the mast. Typically, the fitting needed adapting before use. To work on it meant that I had to have my head and shoulders above the top of the mast; that meant holding on with one hand and balancing to use the other to work. Every time a boat went past, or Bridge or Michala got on or off the boat, the mast would sway a few feet. Surprisingly, after a while, I got used to it and even started to look around and down. I even managed a wave at Michala taking photos of me. The next day we got to try the light out as we sailed down to Porto Calero on the East coast. I had a sense of satisfaction that it worked and was saving me power. It was silly really but I felt good about it. Bridge had bit of a bashing on the way though: firstly he stood in the way of the boom and got a headache; and then he twice moved into the blades of the wind generator. The second time it ripped his t-shirt.

Porto Calero was another toytown. Splendidly kitted out with brass bollards and stainless steel fittings it was a place for rich people to keep their expensive and big yachts. There was a 120 foot yacht called Ghost from Bermuda there. The fenders were bigger than Michala. We looked it up on the web: she has a crew of six but we couldn't find out how much it was to charter her. Safe Arrival looked very old and tatty next to her. The fish were nibbling at the weeds growing on Mildred's steering paddle.

We hired a car to look around Lanzarote. On the West side there is the volcano national park. As we drove into it the landscape suddenly turns to something more akin to the moon, or Mordor. It looked like a cross between a ploughed field on a giant scale and a demolition site. The lava, which had once flowed, had cracked as it cooled just like mud on a hot day at Glastonbury, only this was feet thick in each cracked layer. The brown expanse was very occasionally interrupted with a tiny green plant. As we drove along we spotted a car park. In it were trains of camels loading up their cargoes of tourists for a ride in this desert. We stopped further on for a coach tour where we were taken up though old craters and into lava flows. These were enormous. A later tourist attraction was a man setting fire to brushwood by pushing it over a mini-crater and making geysers by pouring water down funnels nearby. We wondered what his job title would be.

When I had hired the car I was surprised at the lack of things to go through, particularly the petrol level. We found out why: although it was half full when we took it we started to run low as we drove to the north end of the island. After a worried hour of not finding a petrol station a policeman directed us to one. The tank only held twenty litres; it would not have mattered if we had returned it empty. The radio was mad. It would go on or off or change volume with no warning; it would change from drum and base to classical in seconds. No matter what button we pressed it would do its own thing. After an hour of trying different things Michala managed to rip the front off it. At last it was quiet.

Lanzarote has an extremely varied landscape. From the volcanic park we drove through a dramatic change to more irrigated and farmed parts and then to high hills with hairpin bends where the road is hemmed in by a cutting in the rocks. It was almost like the beginning scene of The Italian Job except that we were in a Kia and at ten miles per hour. We reached the cliffs at the north end to look over Graciosa at sunset. I felt a wave of emotion as I looked out to where we had sailed from on our way from Madeira and how we had approached the island a couple of weeks before. I wouldn't be seeing it again. That's one of the things about travelling: the doors open and close so quickly, the chapters are intense but the short lived; my emotions swell and ebb with them.

In a short sail to Rubicon in the south of the island, the next day, we stopped off to anchor and finally managed to get a swim off the boat. We ate out as it was Bridge and Michala's last night. The next morning the taxi picked them up at eight o'clock and they were gone. It felt empty without them. We'd had a lovely week and now all I could do was clean up the boat and wander around planning the next three weeks before Imogen, my daughter, would arrive in Tenerife.

After Bridge and Michala left I moved into a theme of uncertainty. I met up with Ocean Warrior again. They had replaced their engine in Baiona and, because of the delay, had made straight down to the south of Portugal and on to Lanzarote. They had been in Graciosa nearly at the same time as me. They were now unsure of their next move. Various issues meant that they weren't sure whether they would stay the winter in Canaria and journey north to the Azores in Spring; or whether they would cross to the Caribbean. I wasn't sure of my route down to Tenerife. I could travel the East side of Fuerta Ventura, taking in some lesser known areas, or I could head straight for Las Palmas on Grand Canaria. I could even stay in Rubicon for a while.

The ARC had left on the Sunday before. Now that they had gone the rest of us making the crossing were working out our plans. Where would we set off from? With 250 boats having left together it should be quiet in Las Palmas. When would we set off? The trade winds settle after Xmas; general opinion says to leave it until then; the weather forecast agreed. The ARC sailors were being hit by strong head winds; and there were more weather systems on the way. Most of the marinas and anchorages in Canaria are good for NE winds. When it blows from the SW it pushes the Atlantic swells straight in causing uncomfortable and sometimes damaging movement on the pontoons.

I opted for Fuerta Ventura. This gave me a chance to save a bit of money on marinas. I anchored outside Rubicon on the last night. I had a swim around the boat and a deck shower before going ashore for supper on Ocean Warrior. The next morning I had another swim before heading off down to an anchorage on the East coast of this more southerly island. This one was empty. I have got used to cruising around between boats in anchorages, partly to prevent collisions and partly to look at the holding, but here I could pick my spot. I had another swim and shower and went ashore. I got the timing perfect for rowing the dinghy in on the waves but didn't get out of it quick enough. The next wave slapped the side of the dinghy and sent a spray all over me. I was covered in salty water again.

Slightly damp I made for the beach cafe. It was like a Huckleberry Finn shack perched on the shingle at the top of the beach. The foundations were bits of drift wood laid out flat while the walls were bolted down to bits of concrete in the shingle. There were plastic chairs and tables with parasols keeping the late evening sunshine at bay. Colourful, small fishing boats were laid out all around us; and, framed by all this, Safe Arrival sat serenely in the bay. I had meant just to have a coffee but the menu was so good that I had an octopus meal and beer as well; all for twelve euro. In the deepening gloom I rowed back to the boat to sleep. The only problem was that the wind changed twice during the night. Each time it did the chain dragged around to match it. Because anchor drag is a yachtsman's nightmare the noise it makes cuts straight through any sleep. I had another swim the next morning. Finally it seemed as if reality was matching my dreams of cruising. I'd had hot weather, been swimming off the boat and anchored in bays at last.

The weather was due to close in the next day so I headed for the marina at Grand Tarajal. I was welcomed by Mark, a man dressed only in shorts and speaking with an estuary accent. "Yeh mate, bring 'er down the side 'ere. Yeh, sor'ed."He helped me moor up and gave me the low down on the place. I was beginning to realise my classification of marinas. There are the key port types like La Coruna where the business of travelling is catered for in an efficient way. The coming and going of yachts is a daily affair and the services are all set up for effecting repairs and provisioning. Then there is the band of what I have come to call toy town marinas. These come in differing guises but are basically set up for the marina-travelling yotties. They are for the sailors who will leave their yacht in the marina for a couple of months while they go home. These sailors like the convenience that marinas provide; they have electricity, water, clean showers, laundries etc. They can go ashore at any time, pick up wifi from the boat and generally live almost as they do at home. Some of these marinas cater for super-yachts as well. They have varying retail options ashore ranging from a simple bar/restaurant to a complete shopping mall with Henri Lloyd and Musto outlets as well as shops selling vaguely nautical polo shirts and Raybans. These latter usually have a complete range of restaurants. The size of the apartment complex that goes with them depends on the stage they were at when the recession kicked in.

At the bottom end there are the cheap marinas like Grand Tarajal. They attract the impecunious travelers and share the harbour with the fishing fleet. The showers vary in quality from basic to non-existent. Wifi is normally achieved by using a powerful aerial to pick up a local cafe or hotel network. There is a camaraderie amongst the occupants of these marinas. They are normally liveaboards who have made their life on the sea. In this last one I met Mas. He had already made a circumnavigation as well as having kayaked from Denmark to the North Coast of Norway. He was on his way to Antigua for the kite surfing there.

Mark was waiting around for a while to sort out house issues in Portugal. He would be crossing the year after. Mas and another solo sailor, Ian, were waiting for the weather to head south and cross west. I was waiting for the weather to rendezvous with Imogen. We were all waiting, uncertain of when the weather would clear. And each time a system would pass through another appeared on the long range forecast. I could make short dashes but I needed to be certain of a berth in my destination. Mas and Ian though, needed a few days to get far enough south for the systems to miss them.

It was during one of the weather conversations (there were many) that I found out that this unusual weather pattern was responsible for producing massive snow falls in the UK. It seemed bizarre to me that it could be that cold back home. As far as I was concerned the summer had just continued into November. How could it be different? A second thought hit me: it was less than four weeks to the shortest day. How could this be? The sun still set in the mid evening and rose before I woke. I think then that the realisation that this was a year's trip kicked in. Suddenly, I thought of all the feelings I've had and realised that I was living this. I was not on holiday. I would have the same feelings wherever I was. I could be waiting for the weather or I could be waiting for a bus. The impatience would be the same. I could be drinking coffee anywhere. It tasted better in Canaria but apart from that… It may seem obvious, but to me it was a revelation. I thought of all those songs like 'I've been to paradise but never been to me' and a friend telling me once that she found that no matter where she travelled she always took her stuff, her baggage with her. At the time I thought that that was obvious. But that was an intellectual response; now I realised that I needed to do it to know it properly. I felt much more at ease after that. And then, at one of the sundowner sessions, I asked Mas all about his solo sailing and how he copes. He explained that, once settled, on a long passage, he takes his time to do everything properly. He makes sure that he cooks properly, with all the trimmings. He reads, making sure that he's read it all carefully. He carries out maintenance carefully. In doing all this the time becomes vaguely meaningless; it just passes. And, apart from predicting arrival dates, he simply exists. I felt so much better for these two things that I sat down, having put it off for ages, to make my provisioning plans for the crossing. Bring on the Atlantic!

Our little sailing community in Grand Tarajal continued for a few days more. Then, as the weather looked more promising, I began to look towards the next stage. As the others were on much the same path they were thinking much the same thing. The first two set off; really, it was the first three: Michael and Nene had a six month old baby. Michael had been travelling alone from Malta, where he had bought the boat. In Portugal the mast snapped off. While in Berlin, his home city, to sort out finances and do a bit of work, he had met Nene. In a short time she was pregnant and had given up her job as a teacher to go sailing with him. They were on an open ended journey but, at that point, Brazil, via the Cape Verdes, was their next step. It struck me what an extraordinary change she had opted for; to go from stable, "steady" job to peripatetic, liveaboard mother in a year. Like many sailing families, they were easy going. A couple of times we ate with them, all bringing our little contributions.

One night while the wind was still blowing from the South West, the wrong direction, a squall came in. In a matter of seconds it shifted the wind straight into my companionway at a fantastic strength. The accompanying rain shot horizontally straight in. As the swell had been doing the blackout flight simulator thing again I had moved to sleep in the saloon for comfort. Mas and I had been discussing the two tiny drips that come in through my roof earlier that evening. Now, in the middle of a deep sleep I thought that the roof had caved in. I was being showered on. It slowly became apparent to me what was happening. I had no choice but to go up on deck to get the weather boards. So, totally naked, I ran up in the pouring rain and grabbed the boards. Once fitted, I reflected that I had been intending to have a shower in the morning. I hung all the wet stuff up to dry, changed bedding and went back to sleep. In the morning I noticed that the deck bucket had filled by six inches in the night.

The town had fared no better. The topsoil from the volcanic hills had been washed down and on to the pavements, covering them in a brown mud. As the sun came out it cracked up into a crust with slush underneath. In sandals, it reminded me of Glastonbury as I got progressively dirtier feet. Later, it dried completely leaving a layer of dust. That then got blown about by the wind making it difficult for the clean-up operation workers. It also ruined the beach for the few holiday makers left.

The crossing to Las Palmas on Gran Canaria was uneventful but tiring. I set off at midday in light winds down the coast of Fuerta Ventura musing on the way in which we form little communities quickly; and then lose them again just as quickly. In this latter point I was wrong though. A few hours down the coast Mark caught up with me. If his VHF had worked properly we would have had a conversation. As it was we had a shout across the water to find out what route we were both taking. Slowly his boat edged ahead of mine. His was a modern yacht. The same length as mine it had been designed to live in a as well as sail. Two separate cabins, comfy cockpit with large lockers and a sensible galley, it was a very different craft. But the downside was that his was not so comfortable in big seas. He had had a twitchy crossing to Canaria in only a near gale. As we came around the toe of the island there is a wind acceleration zone. This is where the wind is diverted and funneled around by high hills of the island. Although the sea was relatively flat, the wind got up to a stiff breeze and we had a boisterous few hours from sunset. Then it dropped off a bit but the rolling waves that had formed kept on going. It felt like there was no wind, because the boat was rolling around with the sails flapping and snapping at the deck fittings, but I was still doing four knots. Although I was not feeling at all sea sick, down below was not a comfortable place to be. I set the alarm to go off every fifteen minutes, made up a cosy bed and tried to sleep. With the thoughts of a shipping lane to cross and land to hit on the other side I had no difficulty in waking up each time; and, later, I got to sleep easily each time too.

Las Palmas is the largest city in the Canary Islands. The lights of the city were visible from miles off giving the impression that I was very close. Slowly, it became clear where the harbour was. Large container ships were congregating there. I had to make my way between them, listening to their conversations on the radio. As I got nearer I realised how unused to large cities I have become. It just grew and grew to take up the whole of my horizon; the orange street lights rising on the hills and the car headlights swing flashes all about. Somewhere in this lot was a green light that flashed every five seconds; but where? I constantly swept the horizon with the binoculars for it; it eventually appeared from behind a docking ship. At last I could shape my course with some certainty although it was complicated by all the ships at anchor. They show their deck lights at night for visibility but this makes it difficult to see that they don't have any navigation lights on. I had to assume they were under way until certain. Exhausted from concentration, I moored at the first pontoon I could find.

Once checked in and sorted the next morning I took stock of the marina. It was enormous, the size of all the marinas in the Hamble pushed together with those in the Solent. There must have been thousands of yachts there. The marina office had a continuous stream of people checking in while the narrow entrance was a potential collision point for all the traffic each way during the day. I had moved from a small one man show town, to a big city marina, literally. One of the receptionists reminded me of an Aardman giraffe. She had a long neck and was very expressive in her Spanish way. When I arrived she was attending to a young, confident, English skipper of a super yacht. Her head bobbed about on her long neck as if she was on strings while she pulled a variety of pleasing smiles. When he left a middle-aged woman took his place. There was a slight problem in her account. The giraffe was not happy about this. Her neck retracted and she pulled a series of mouths that indicated displeasure, like a school teacher with a slightly naughty child that she expected more of. Then she tilted her head on one side while not saying anything or looking at her customer. There was a standoff for a moment or two while the customer said nothing; and then the giraffe's hands came out from under the desk to tap the keyboard just slightly harder than was necessary.

Later, when I had walked the couple of kilometres around this enormous marina to collect the wifi password that they hadn't given me, I got cross with her. I had been standing, waiting for her attention while she was on the phone when she told me they were closed. "Come back at four o'clock" she said with her neck disappearing like a turtle. At that point I explained in a firm but angry voice that I had been overcharged, made to wait for ages, had walked around the marina for nothing and that I wanted her to give me the wifi password now and that then I would not bother them again. Amazingly, she smiled, the neck emerged and she graciously ordered her minion to give the password immediately.

Still tired and not entirely certain of myself in this large place I decided to leave exploration for a day or so. As I was berthing I had noticed Michael and Nene on the next pontoon so I visited them. And then Mark appeared in his dinghy to inform us that Ian was also here, anchored outside. While wandering around I met other boats from the last few weeks. This is the last staging post; the final all round sorting-out place before the crossing, no matter which way we are headed. For now we are on the frontier, the edge of the Atlantic. From now on we watch the horizon; trepidation, for a long time deep inside, was now pacing the bars, just out of sight. There was a sense of frustration, expectancy and inertia in all the conversations. Some are trying to get to Antigua before Xmas. Others have no time schedule but want to move on. Some, like me, had no intention of leaving until after Xmas. For most it was the first time crossing the Atlantic; we were facing a great unknown. We all watched the forecasts, watching the lows being pushed south to form head winds or, at least, kill the favourable trade winds. Soon we too would set off to cross the point of no return.

While I was wandering around Las Palmas I was struck by the similarity with La Coruna. Both are on headlands surrounded by beaches. At first it is confusing because I left the sea behind me only to find it now in front. The architecture in Las Palmas was much less decorative than La Coruna; someone told me that it was more South American than European. Most of it is cheap concrete slab buildings. The streets are on a grid system but with forty five degree roads cutting through. It felt, walking through, as if great big cheese slices have been shoved together.

I walked into the city from the marina. Immediately, I had to climb a big hill and then down again. On the other side I found the tourist beach; a long sweep of sand and a long promenade to keep it company. The tourists sat out on the cafe sweeps while, only two streets in, the Spanish got on with whatever they had to get on with. The two seemed almost unaware of each other. On the way back I headed to the docks end of the harbour. I entered a Soho-like area with bars, night clubs, sex shops, cheap, but good, restaurants and Chinatown. And just like Soho there was a Corte Ingles within a couple of hundred metres.

On one street I recognised the three Swedes from La Coruna. But now they were four; Tomas had joined them for the Atlantic crossing. The three were all healthy coloured, blonde and tanned, while he was a pasty white with tinges of red. I wondered what it must be like to join an established group for this marathon. They were off soon. They had been waiting to fix their engine in Las Palmas for four weeks and were desperate to go; even if this meant starting into a head wind. They came around for a beer in the afternoon before they left. I felt quite envious of them. I was excited too; the big part of the adventure was starting for them. Mine would be soon.

Only a few days after I had arrived, an English boat came on to my pontoon. It transpired that they had been in the ARC but had retired. After nearly two weeks they still had had two thousand miles to go. Some of the crew had cut off dates, appointments and so, and continuing would have gone past these. They told us of boats getting low on food and water; decisions of whether to continue in light winds or large, sloppy seas; and the frustration of it all. That's the problem of sailing to deadlines – we may have been frustrated in Las Palmas but at least we were waiting on dry land and not, like the ARC, trying to fit into transport timetables; fighting the gods of circumstance.

Nene and Michael and I hired a car to explore the island. We went into the old town of Las Palmas first. That was a mistake as Nene spotted a hippy, Indian clothing shop. That meant a lot of trying clothes on and opinions being sought. I was happy though as I found a cafe to get my morning hit of coffee. Michael was very good too; he was very patient and then offered to buy her a dress as a Xmas present. Christopher Columbus visited these islands a lot in his travels. Practically everywhere there is some monument to something he did while somewhere here. In Las Palmas there is a house belonging to the town dignitaries that he visited on each occasion. Now it is a museum to him. There is a full size model of what they think his cabin would have looked like. The rest of the house is more about getting an idea of what houses looked like then. Very nice; and there are a couple of McCaws in the courtyard garden too. There was a sign warning visitors to be careful and a picture of a finger being bitten. In the little art gallery, mainly of the islands' only renaissance artist, there was the only picture I have ever seen of the virgin Mary looking like a young, attractive girl.

On we went to a small town half way up the mountain. Gran Canaria is essentially a round, inactive volcano poking out of the Atlantic. After finding our way up to some altitude we found it just as Lonely Planet had described: a restored town centre but in a traditional and sympathetic way. The tapas bar in the square was moderately trendy but not out of place. The woman who served us was lovely; she heated up some baby milk for us; she forgot the orders; and she took hours to bring the food. The food was delicious. All this meant that, by the time we got towards the top of the mountain the sunset was near. However, this didn't affect us much; the clouds had assembled to obscure the view for the summit. Even if it had been clear we wouldn't have seen anything. There was a rock fall blocking the road. We were waved back down.

On the way back down we detoured to a little town on the North East corner of the island to visit a friend of Michael's from their time in Algeria. Veit's boat was out of the water next to the ferry terminal. They had limited wifi access as it depended on when the ferry was in dock. When it was they could pick up the passengers' network but when it sailed they were out of range. Veit and Sophie had been travelling for over fifteen years but only relatively recently moved onto the water. The boat was open plan; well open; any form of planning seemed to be entirely accidental. That was the way they lived their lives; they would wander from place to place in time-free travel toward anywhere that provided diving or climbing. They had three other friends visiting at the same time as us. Totally unfazed by these surprise visits they managed to provide chai tea and a rice meal for us. It took some time to find out which floorboards the rice was stored under, and some more time to find utensils (chopsticks) to eat with but, eventually, we all perched around the various forms of seating arrangement to eat. It reminded me of times visiting friends in squats in London when I was a teenager; meandering and happy chaos; an antidote to the organised, rush of modern life. And I thought that all that life style had gone.

The Saturday was looking like there would be a weather window to depart for the crossing and several yachts were going to take the opportunity. Ian decided to hold a goodbye party for them on his fifty foot steel motor cruiser: Celtic Spray. It was big enough to take several families and other assorted crews comfortably for an evening. The sense of camaraderie gets high at these occasions when people who have got to know each other quite well over a few days or weeks say goodbye with no clear idea if they will ever meet again. Email addresses, routes and last minute notes are swapped along with potential points of paths crossing again. On this occasion there were two newbies to sailing asking lots of questions. Dirk and Virginie, two Belgians, had been wandering the pontoons looking for crewing opportunities with no luck. They had been about to sleep on the beach when Ian took them in for the night. In the course of the next day he found out that they were hard working and fun. He also got recommendations from the ship they had crossed on from Tenerife. In the middle of all the talk about how they could improve their chances, they were handing out posters advertising themselves. Ian took one, looked at it and ripped it up. There was a moment of horror on everyone's faces

"No need for that" he said. "You've got your slots on this boat."Incredulous looks were quickly changed to exclamations of delight. We were all pleased that this couple had their crossing sorted. After that the evening took on a cosy blur.

Things continued in Las Palmas much the same. The days were fairly leisurely, with slow preparations for the crossing, and usually ended with sundowners on someone's boat. The cruise liners that I had got to know in Madeira came and went with their loud, three long blasts when they were leaving. They felt like old friends.

Over the journey I have been regretting not taking up an offer from a friend. She had offered me her folding bike for the year. I had refused, partly because it was so new and worth a bit, but also because I was overwhelmed by preparations for the journey. Over the weeks I have been envious of people who disappear for a long ride and see much more of the countries visited than I do. In Las Palmas I managed to acquire a bike. Suddenly my wandering range from the marina increased. It was a tatty, folding mountain bike. I'm not sure I would have wanted to go anywhere near a mountain with it but for the city it was good. I shared it with the young girl on the same pontoon as me. After a few days she asked where I had put it. Surprised I said I hadn't moved it. Someone had stolen it from under my nose while I was sitting chatting on the boat; or maybe the original owner had taken it back.

I got news of Rusty from the two French sailors I had met in Gijon. Rusty had finally left for Antigua a week or so before. The Frenchmen had sorted their gearbox trouble, sailed to La Gomera and then the engine had played up. Then their dinghy was lost so they were on the way up to Lanzarote to buy a cheap one.

I had organised to meet my daughter, Imogen, in Tenerife but the winds had been against me. These winds would also mean that the marinas over there would be uncomfortable. We rearranged for her to fly to Las Palmas instead. I have realised that it is good fun to meet people at airports. I had met Hazel in Santiago de Compostela and Bridge and Michala in Aricife; but it was brilliant to meet Imogen. I was excited and all day I had to keep checking the clocks to make sure I wasn't going to be late. I had wanted to give her a sun and beach holiday but as we were in Las Palmas it had to be a sun and city one instead. There are no anchorages near where we could have visited for the day, or where we could have dropped the hook for the night, because the wind was blowing straight into them. It would have been too uncomfortable. I showed her the city and introduced her to Spanish culture as much as I know of it. On the first night, in the restaurant, I impressed her with my command of Spanish. I had to admit that I all I was doing was listing our menu choice to the waiter. We hired a car and went up to the mountain again. On the way we stopped off at a hot and dusty canyon. It went on for miles up and up into the mountains. Each corner looked like it must be the end but we just kept on driving on. At a car park we stopped and looked around a little village. The houses are built into the rock. They have normal little gardens in front of normal front doors. Some of the gates had pigs, chickens, sheep or ducks in the caves behind them. There are narrow pavements/paths running between them that we could walk along. To add to the bizarre visage there were Father Christmas models abseiling from higher rocks down to the doorways. It had the feel of the SAS dropping in for a charity event at a city farm.

A couple of times during the day we stopped in a small town or village for refreshments. It was nice to sit in small bars, observing life and chatting. She is at university. She told me about her life there and her ideas for plans. She also told me all about her coursework. It is a funny feeling to be taught by my children. I remember it from when my son started to tell me about marketing and theology. It is a change of role; for twenty od years I had been guiding, advising and imparting knowledge. Now they were on their own paths and I am an equal recipient of their knowledge. I listened and learnt a lot about nineteenth century literature. At least I had just been listening to Nicholas Nickleby on talking book so I had some reference point. We chewed the cud over a large number of cups of cafe con leche for me and cafe lecheleche for her. This latter is the same but for the addition of a small amount of condensed milk. It sounds awful but tastes really nice.

Her stay rocketed by. Before I knew it I was travelling back to the airport with her. I was very sad to see her go. I wouldn't see her again for at least six months. That's longer than when I dropped her off when she worked her ski season. She was my last visitor. After her I was going on possibly the most challenging journey of my life. Before I saw her again I would have travelled nearly seven thousand miles; about ten weeks on my own at sea. She was my last organised anchor point; from then on any visits were going to be chance and last minute arrangements.

Back on the boat it seemed empty. There was none of her stuff lying about. I was lonely. I'd got used to having her around. I got a text message. It was from my ex-wife. She said that Imogen was slowly recovering from the shock of landing in minus five degrees. It occurred to me that, before every other sea passage, every other visitor had been accompanied by fair winds. Before Chris arrived to cross Biscay and Janet arrived to cross to Madeira the winds had been perfect only for them to turn foul as they arrived. While Imogen had stayed the winds had been unfavourable. On checking the forecast it looked like they would be good a few days later. The whole Marina watched the forecasts in anticipation. With one week to Xmas no one, despite the fairy light palm trees and the carols, was thinking about presents or shopping. That had no relevance and didn't make sense. They were in thirty one degrees and getting excited about leaving for another continent on the other side of an ocean.

9 THE CROSSING

Preparations continued as a weather window became more and more obvious for Wednesday. I organised a party on the quayside but it was not too wild. Some of the party moved on to Marco's boat. He and his family have lived here for three years while his wife, Lisbeth, does some accountancy courses. Marco is African French and Lisbeth Spanish. Somehow salsa dancing came into the conversation and it turned out that they loved dancing but had no music. I gave them a salsa CD I'd made and we danced the night away, precariously balanced on various semi-horizontal sections of his boat. Meanwhile, Sergio, my neighbour, did conjuring tricks which, try as we might, we could not fathom. A good night; Lizbeth has since told me that, despite many parties, it is that one they remember.

The next evening, my last, I spent on Gaia, a Faroes boat. This life has brought home to me the strength of humanity that can exist. Here we were, Germans, Faroes, English, Hungarian, French and Danish, all having fun together, offering hospitality and help, while perhaps never meeting again. Earlier, I had had possession of an iPhone for two hours. Ricardo, someone I met in a bar, could not charge his iPhone. I told him I had a charger so he'd brought it to my boat, left it while it charged, and then called back later. I'm not sure that would happen in a bar in the UK.

I wanted to get drunk with them on Gaia. They were having so much fun but I had to leave the next day and it is not good to start a passage with a hangover. The Faroes tradition seems to be to get your guests as drunk as possible, and, if they refuse one of the drinks, then they drink it themselves. We tried some Welsh single malt. The Brits had never heard of this before so pronounced it to be sheep's piss. I had to try that; actually it was quite nice, a sort of poor man's Jura.

Leaving Day. It had really arrived. I took Randi, from Gaia, for a breakfast of chocolate and churros, did a last minute shop and started to get the boat ready. It somehow didn't feel real. And then Ian from Celtic Spray came past to say that he had a lift to the Frontera Police so he could check out from immigration officially. I could go too. That helped make it more real and it only took a few minutes; then back to the boat and more readiness preparation. At the last minute I decided that I would buy a harness for my life line rather than use the life jacket. It has no bulk to get in the way and, if I went overboard, the life jacket would only prolong my demise. I would be able to watch Safe Arrival keep going without me for a while longer. I had a last European coffee and undid the lines.

I only had one line undone when the world of Las Palmas yotties seemed to descend on my pontoon. I had help from all quarters. Shouts of good luck went up and echoed around the pontoons. I felt quite emotional. I tooted my horn like the cruise ships and got replies echoing across the sea of masts. I could see Ian and his crew getting ready too. They looked up and shouted good luck too. I can still recall the washing machine of emotions that ran through me as I passed them on the last pontoon. "I must be f***ing mad" I shouted to them as I turned to leave the harbour. I set the foresail and the wind took me out of the docks and down the coast. My solo adventure had begun.

There was a strong wind and a big swell so I moved off fast. Fast in yachting terms; three hours later Las Palmas began to shrink away in the haze. I avoided all the big ships at anchor off the coast and set a course to get me around the headland. I kept wondering what I was doing. I kept getting all sorts of aches and pains. I'm sure this was my rational self trying to create reasons for turning back. I talked to myself out loud: "This is the beginning of an amazing experience. Three hours out of 28 days gone and you'll get used to it." And then I heard the radio; a boat that had started an hour before me had alternator problems and was turning back. That seemed to be the jolt I needed to settle down to the journey. I'd prepared lots of food so I didn't need to cook on the first day. I just munched and thought about what I was doing and what I needed to prepare for. The first night I slept fitfully and saw the occasional ship.

At daylight I was hot and grumpy. I wondered if this was caffeine withdrawal. I'd had no coffee for twenty four hours. It took me ages to get the sails sorted as the wind slowly dropped to a slow pace. The clouds had closed in. I saw a sail in the distance. After a snooze it was much closer, I thought I saw someone waving on the deck so I turned around; but then they radioed me. The waving was them chasing after their two year old who had run up the deck without his life jacket on! They, "Ouma," had had engine problems but had fixed them (they thought.) We stayed close by all night. With the lack of wind and sunshine both of us ran our batteries down. I motored for a couple of hours the next morning to charge up while they jury-rigged their fuel supply, the real engine problem.

The good thing about this meeting was that they told me about the Rum Runners Net. This is a social net on the shortwave radio where all the crossing yachts check in each morning to make sure everyone is ok; and to exchange weather conditions and sailing expertise. Ouma learned from it how to keep their engine going while they changed course to Cabo Verde where another yacht had also altered course. The other yacht, listening in, had realised that they had the spare part that Ouma needed. They had offered to turn back slightly easterly and south to meet them in Cabo Verde where they could hand it over. Such is the brotherhood of the sea. It being Christmas Day it made a nice present for them. My Christmas present was from some dolphins: they came and played, jumping and spinning, around the boat for an hour. There were loads of them for a good 200 metres around. As they surface they make a little snorting noise that I got to know well, often during the night.

After that I settled into a routine. I'd wake up at daylight, check the fresh food for signs of going off, do the maintenance checklist and then listen to the net. Steering problems and other engine problems seemed to be the main issues for the other boats. I was envious of those who checked in so far ahead of me. They had only 200 miles to go when I had over 2000. I'd plan the day: what was I going to eat, when was I going to read. I'd check the winds with what had been reported on the net and I'd also lose hours at a time just running thoughts. Sometimes I'd manage to jot them down but often I find two hours had gone by without my knowing what I'd been thinking about. I'd cook supper before the sun set around six o'clock and then listen to a talking book and an album while watching the stars. One night I listened to Bob Dylan, "Blood on the Tracks" and thought about all the relationships I'd had. Under the stars I realised how beautiful these songs were. A lot of them are about lost relationships. These stayed with me overnight sometimes. One morning I woke in tears, sobbing. I must have been crying for some time as my pillow was wet. I couldn't remember my dream but I knew it was about Julia, a relationship from more than two years before. Over the years that we'd lived together she had encouraged me to do things, to be active. She'd introduced me to the outdoor activities club. I'd taken up skiing, paddling, mountain walking with her. Over several years we'd had an intense relationship. I wasn't worried about crying. I wasn't choking back the tears. In a strange way it felt very comfortable, like the sun's warmth on a cloudy day. Part of me was surprised. I'd always felt that crying was a terrain to cross before returning to normal. I'd never felt it to be something just to accept before. Here I was, happily crying while getting on with my life aboard. Amidst this it occurred to me that there was some bizarre symmetry to Charles Ryder's Atlantic crossing. Bed time was around 10pm. During the night I would wake up at regular intervals to check all was OK. Often I would stay up in the cockpit, maybe listening to more music, looking at the stars. Despite the constant movement, the roll of the boat, the waves passing under, I had a sense of peace, deep and content; there, vastly insignificant, my world was alright.

It never occurred to me that I could get jet lag while travelling so slowly. I was now moving significantly west. Every 700 miles or so was worth one hour forward on the clock; the sun would rise and set an hour later. I've often noticed, in the UK, that the clocks going back make people tired for a week. Now I was doing it every week. The Rum Runners Net did not change time though; they kept to ten o'clock UTC. As I crossed and altered the clocks this became earlier so by the end of the passage it was at six in the morning. That meant setting the alarm to hear it and then going back to bed after. By this time I was wondering if it was worth it. I was on the home run, most of the check ins were from people I didn't know and the reception got poorer the further west I got; and maybe it wasn't jet lag but just tiredness from working the passage.

The first two weeks the wind was often light. I would need the spinnaker up just to go faster than a dawdle. I would procrastinate about raising it. I would check the wind carefully. It took half an hour to set it. I didn't want to go through all that only to have to take it down again. If the wind got up I'd be in trouble. It is a powerful sail; getting it flying was easy but getting it down could be difficult in a strong wind. That was always on my mind. I would take it down before dusk as I couldn't risk having to get it down at night. When I did take it down the boat slowed down and then the swell could catch up with me. There was a light swell from the north east plus one from the south east too. Every now and then both of them would catch the stern at the same time. The boat would lurch one way and heel over only to do the same the other way immediately after. Usually, this would happen just as I was spreading the marmalade on toast or dishing out the last component of a meal. The toast, or the rice, would fly off the plate and on to the floor. Eventually, I started eating out of the saucepan. It was safer.

The light winds also made me conservation conscious. Apart from the electric, I needed to make sure I didn't run out of water. I started washing up in sea water, I didn't shave and I saved on washing by wearing hardly any clothes. I had my first shower on New Year's Day; the black bag solar shower that I'd filled up in Las Palmas had been sitting heating up in the sun everyday; now it was to be part used. I thought of all the times I have been nursing a hangover on this day and wondered what all my friends were doing. It felt wonderful to be clean – and I'd not had a drop of alcohol for over a week – nor coffee neither. But not shaving was horrible; by two weeks in I could not splash my face to wake up and feel good. The water just ran off my beard. And every time I had a drink I had to rinse my moustache after. By three weeks I'd had enough and shaved it off. Boy did that feel good. It had never occurred to me that I could shave at sea; on single overnight passages I'd never got that used to the motion. Now I had been on a moving platform for so long that I couldn't remember what stillness was. I'd so acclimatised to the motion that I could happily guide a razor over my face without any worry.

Half way across I caught my only fish. This was the first bite since the abortive tuna on the way to Graciosa. I was just so happy to land it. I recognised it as a barracuda from when James and I visited the fish market in Aricife. It looked somewhat bemused and a bit embarrassed as I dropped it on to the cockpit floor. I poured some whisky into its gills to put it to sleep painlessly; and then I cut it up. I had enough for three meals. Having caught it just before lunch I was eating it within thirty minutes of catching it. It was delicious. I felt good about that all day.

After that I thought that I'd got fishing sussed. I put this wonderful lure out a couple of days later and thought about lunch. When the line went taught I was excited for a moment. But immediately it went taught there was a slight pause, a big judder and a slack line. It had broken the twenty two kilogram line. Whatever it was that I had caught was very big, and I would not have wanted it in the cockpit. I'd heard a story from the German couple in Graciosa about catching a Marlin. Once in the cockpit it thrashed about so much that it managed to flip down the companionway and into the saloon. There its thrashing trashed the wooden interior. It was a good story even if unlikely. For me it was another lure lost. I had to start making them but I never got the hang of how to attach them to the lines properly. I lost every one. I vowed to pick an expert's brain once across.

Once past the half-way mark I found the wind. From then on the spinnaker was redundant as I took more and more reefs in. Now I was fairly flying; it was no longer about how much sail could I put out but how much I could afford not to take in a reef at night. One evening I got it wrong; somewhere around midnight I had to don a head torch to go up to the mast and reduce sail. I thought about it, questioning if I really needed to do it, for about ten minutes before I got to grips with myself. I was scared but I was going to have to do it. I climbed out of the cockpit, head torch shining on the narrow deck between the cabin and the dark sea. The sparkling reflections from the guard rail and my safety line made it difficult to see past them; beyond seemed blackness. Up at the mast it wasn't as bad as I thought it would be but I was still glad to get back to the safety of the cockpit. I once went to hear Dee Caffari talk. At the end I remembered asking her about solo sailing. She'd said that I would get to know myself very well, and that I'd only once leave it late to shorten sail. She was right.

The sound of the water passing the hull, at this new speed, was a constant, light roar. I often thought of those Hitchcock movies on a train; towards the end of a scene the camera will draw back to the roar of the wheels on the tracks as the train rushes on into the night. It was a constant reminder of the travel; day after day after day. I began to believe that I might get there in less than twenty eight days. I passed the three-quarter way point a day early. I was excited by this until I realised that, even at this new speed, the next days would be the same. The sea would still be empty and the land beyond sight tomorrow and the day after that and the day after. Any day after tomorrow means forever. It was beyond my time frame. I got fed up with the sea. I wanted some wind from the side; not always off the stern. I complained about the rolling of the boat; the lean one way and then the other all the way from Las Palmas.

And then I remembered two things: one was a talk by Debra Searle, the woman who rowed the Atlantic solo after her husband had to be extracted. She had a phrase: "choose your attitude." I suddenly thought: "I've chosen to do this. This is my dream. I'm lucky to be here." And then I laughed. 'Living the dream' is made up of two parts: the dream may be great but I still had to live. And I remembered Mas and doing everything as best I could and let the time become irrelevant. I was travelling faster than I'd predicted and I was fed up? At this I planned and cooked a really good meal. I'd celebrate with some quality. I suppose it was relative quality as I was just about out of fresh produce; but it made for a good end to most of the vegetables.

I also thought about travelling. The constant newness of each destination is exhausting. I'd noticed that I regularly returned to the thought of the home run, back up the Bristol Channel. I wondered if this was because this would be the next familiar part of the trip. I'd moved on from living in the spaces between the paving stones to almost removing the stones altogether. I was living in a space thirty two feet by ten feet surrounded by over 2000 miles of water. Apart from the other sailors dotted around this ocean, the closest people would be those in the

Space Lab. Did they listen to VHF channel 16? On this note I decided that, once I was in Grenada, I would spend at least a fortnight in one place, to get used to the country and the new culture.

This new fortitude was severely tested shortly after that. When checking the water tank, in the bilges, I found sea water all around it. I traced the leak to the stern gland. This is where the propeller shaft goes through the hull. It was leaking at about two drops per second. I'd taken in about twenty litres since yesterday. I could cope with this but I didn't really want to be pumping out at that rate. In the boat maintenance bible it showed how to replace the packing tape that seals the leak but I had two problems: firstly, there was NO WAY that I was going to take the old one out while 1000 miles from land. The second was that I didn't have any packing tape. Eventually, I found out that there was no grease in the pump; the packing tape was not being greased and it had contracted. I refilled the pump and the problem was solved.

On days twenty one and twenty two I tried to work out what my arrival time would be while, at the same time, trying not to get too excited. As the wind died away the next night I worked out that I could motor and get there the next afternoon. After a snooze I came on deck to watch the sunrise. In the gloomy, cloud covered dawn I noticed that the mainsail was an odd shape. Sometimes the reefing lines can get caught up in the sail but they were free. The mainsail had ripped right across just under the third reef. How had this happened with no wind? And then I remembered: it was centred to dampen the roll of the boat. During my snooze I'd heard a sound like the cracking of those folded paper hats that we used to crack like whips as kids. It must have ripped as the boat rolled.

I looked behind me to see a rainy squall, my first one. The wind can get up to gale force in squalls. I needed to get the sail away quickly before the wind got up and tore the rip all the way. Once tied down I looked on the bright side: it had waited until I was nearly there and it was only the stitching on a seam. If it had gone earlier it would have made the journey far harder. Changing to the spare mainsail on a rolling boat is not easy.

I remembered the old sayings about not being safe until the journey is completely finished and people doing strange things when tired. So I planned the last few hours. I looked out all the charts for Grenada, cooked and ate, cleared up all the lines, prepped the anchor and then had a shave, used the last solar shower water and put on new clothes. I turned on the VHF; almost straight away there was an announcement about the Grenada Hash House Harriers run that night. That was too soon for me but I made a note to run with them another time. My first contact with other people for all this time and it was from one of the most socially organised groups around.

In the gloom of the squall that had now passed me I saw a vague silhouette of land; this must be Grenada. Suddenly the sun came out and it turned to bright green; my first green since Las Palmas. Once oriented to the coast I called up my contacts there. The response was from another boat, Wendy, on Meringue. She explained that Bev and Mike were on a charter job but had asked her to welcome me. It's true that sailors regard the sea as safe and land as dangerous. After more than three weeks I started to concentrate. There were rocky fingers sticking out from the coast and some submerged rocks off shore. Repeatedly checking the charts I navigated around the headland. There was the bay. All over were boats at anchor. There must have been over seventy of them. While preparing the anchor I weaved my way to where Wendy had suggested dropping it, near De Big Fish bar. After two goes at anchoring, I turned the motor off in Prickly Bay, Grenada. I had taken just over twenty four days to sail just nearly 2 900 miles. I was there.

I was putting the boat to bed when Wendy came over to greet me. "Have a beer" I ordered. "I've carried these all the way from Las Palmas and I'm not drinking alone!" We sat there while I gabbled at her, my first listener for three weeks, and she filled me in on the way things worked around here. I couldn't remember much of anything she said when I tried to think of it later though.

She took me to the customs office but I'd read the times wrong. They'd just closed. She'd forgotten the key to her dinghy lock so she suggested I got a coffee while she got a lift back to her boat. As she went I realised that I had no money. I couldn't buy any coffee. Later, once I got the dinghy out and had got ashore, I walked to the cashpoint a mile away in the heat. All the traffic tooted at me. Calls of "taxi?" came flying at me. All the traffic was rushing past and I could smell the strong petrol. My senses were overloaded; after weeks of blue sky, blue sea, no conversations, no people and no smells this new land was overpowering. A few years earlier, in Cuba, we had found that there was usually a sting, albeit very nice, when we were approached. Here, in Grenada, people were saying 'hi' from all around. The local taxis and busses were tooting at me because that's what they do. But I didn't have any money. It was hot and I wasn't used to walking, or shoes. My brain was frazzling. I wanted them all to go away.

At last I came to the cashpoint. How much did I need? It didn't matter; it rejected me. A mile further on I found another; this one told me I was not authorised. Oh. My phone was on the boat. I walked back to De Big Fish and booked a table for one while hoping that I could sort this out with the bank. Otherwise I would have no money, no food and no fun.

The very nice people at the bank in the UK apologised profusely, reversed the charges and sorted it out. I went back ashore, had some more beer, ate my meal, emailed my arrival to my friends and, over the next three hours, soaked up the bar, the band and the atmosphere. It felt good. I was on my own, surrounded by people, but happy just to absorb the sounds of conversation. I rowed back to the boat where I could sleep in the forepeak cabin again. I could sleep all night again. I could have the hatch open again. I was here. I was in the Caribbean. I had arrived. I'd done it. I'd really done it.

10 GRENADA TO ST LUCIA

I'm in the Caribbean. I'm in the Caribbean. I'm really in the Caribbean. I'd crossed the Atlantic! It took me ages to get my head around this. I'd actually opened the portfolio of charts for this side of the Atlantic. I'd really used them. It took me ages to get up and ages to get breakfast. Changing routine, from the daily passage chores, from that simple existence to planning a day seemed insurmountable.

I went over to customs in the dinghy. They were housed on the top floor of a two-storey, Huckleberry Finn type shack. The bottom half is a laundry and a gas bottle top up place. There was a French crew already in there; they asked me what a stowaway was. One of the questions was "Did you have any stowaways on board; if so how many?" I remembered this question as being hilarious before I left but, now, on the health-screening form it seemed perfectly normal. The customs workers were pleasant; they pottered through the various forms and talked quietly in patois. I was never sure if they were talking to me or not but I got processed. Then I tried to pay by card. Not possible. I had to take the dinghy all the way back to the other landing point, walk back to the banks and get some money. Then I walked all the way back and crossed to pay. After all this I sat outside the other bar on this side of the bay, drinking coffee and taking it all in again.

As I rowed the dinghy back to the boat I was approached by a tall man in a dinghy. This was Mike. He and Bev had just got back from a charter job. He invited me over to supper that evening. I first heard of Mike and Bev when a colleague showed me some photos. She was being taken down the Avon, from Bristol to Portishead, on a catamaran. I was very envious at the time. When she heard that I was going to Grenada she effected an introduction by email. They moved here a couple of years ago and have put down roots, as far as you can put roots down from a catamaran, in Prickly Bay. They do chartering and general 'fixit' work here. I had a lovely evening with them and felt like we were old friends by the time I went home to bed. We'd swapped stories about our crossings. I told them about running out of yeast so having to make pan bread, the fifty two plus boats on the crossing net; and mending George, the tiller pilot with a spot of glue. They had been as dismayed as I was about the Southern Cross. I had been expecting something of awe, not a tiny splodge of four stars.

Bev organised that she would take me into St Georges the next day. After the cruisers' net, I picked her up and we went ashore. It turned out that I had walked half way there the day before. We got on the reggae bus. I think Bristol could learn from this service. The government set the route (well the principal of the route anyway) and the cost. Then two guys will get a minibus; add a high-volume sound system, and drive them both at full power. One will drive as the other conducts. How this works is that they both scan any pedestrian for the slightest inkling that they may want to take the bus. Then the driver will hoot the horn and slow the bus while the conductor calls out of the sliding side door. As there are many pedestrians this is a continuous activity. Anyone can start up their bus service so there is one every minute; or maybe two. There is also an attempted Tardis principle: a bus is never full; there is always space for one more fare in a quickly folded out new seat.

As the yottie population land at "De Big Fish" the bus route often diverts down there. We caught our bus twenty metres from the dinghy. I began to go into overwhelm. Bev kept trying to tell me things but they were leaving by the other ear just as soon as she said them. The close proximity of so many people; the sounds, the heat, the smells, the colour; it all seemed like a carnival, not a normal day. Apart from the Spice Market feeling a bit touristy, it was all authentic. We bought fruit from traders in the street and I manage to persuade Bev to go up to the castle. Here I tried to imagine a gunship shelling this small, unprotected city, the size of Dartmouth, during the American intervention nearly thirty years ago. I just couldn't imagine it.

St Georges is built around a natural double harbour. The buildings at the waterfront could be out of Georgian England. There were a mixture of cruise liners, yachts, fishing boats and cargo ships around. The hills behind are covered in steep streets and buildings leading up into the green hills behind. These are more sparsely populated. Some buildings had no roof. They, including the Houses of Parliament's, were removed by Hurricane Ivan about six years ago.

We had rotis for lunch. A roti is like a large envelope; a cross between a pancake and a wrap, sealed all around and, with, traditionally, vegetables but nowadays, various fillings. This, with one beer and I was falling asleep.

We met Mike who had to renew his driving license. This involved an hour in an office housed between the fire station and the police station. While he was in there I sat outside and watched the comings and goings. Almost everyone in Grenada is very friendly and the calls of "hey mon, enjoying de cool" were frequent as I sat in the shade, in a doorway and next to the chickens, who appeared to be part of the fire station. The woman who I knew to be sorting Mike out kept walking back and forth across the yard. I wondered how Mike was getting on. It turned out that he'd had to go and get some photos and other bits and then the payment machine had broken down. So he had to go back to try again another day.

Bev introduced me to the Mount Aries Reading Scheme where cruisers go up to the rural area of Mt Aries and help with children's' reading. The idea is good, and, as a social project, it goes a lot further than just reading, but it was strange to be listening to a Grenadian kid read from a ladybird book about Peter and Jane on holiday on a Devon beach. I'm not sure it made any sense to him at all. The system of rote learning used, I think, meant that they recognised the words but the context was missing. There had been some attempts to improve this but it needed a wholesale change and commitment. As passing cruisers we were not in position to do this. Someone had once tried to introduce Harry Potter but the stories of witchcraft had not gone down well.

The first week seemed to be a series of meeting new people. I tidied up enough not to feel embarrassed when people visited, went for a swim each morning and evening and spent the rest of the days chatting with others. Yanina was a Warrior 35; the type of boat I had considered for the trip. Bob and Liz had heard my call for a spare wind generator blade and invited me aboard. They had a whole set of them so they gave me two. They'd been given theirs. I needed one because, when Nick from Mariposa had been visiting, I'd walked into the wind generator. The blades are designed to break before injury but I had a scar for some time after that. Each morning the cruisers net has a 'services required' section. Within a few seconds of asking for a blade I had several offers. What a community.

One night in the bar I got chatting with a five year old called JJ. When Bev arrived she was so enchanted with him that we found his parents to say hello. Geoff was an American doctor who worked sometimes in the US Virgin Islands. He and his wife had decided to buy a catamaran and go off, with their three kids, doing bits of work occasionally. We had a fascinating conversation about the pros and cons of leaving the conventional educational system for a life on the waves. They had left the tick box mentality, the way American education has gone, for the life skills of sailing cruising.

It was interesting to be sharing a world with Americans, neither of us being in our own country. It shows some of the national characteristics. The Brits will go anywhere if someone suggests it while the Americans will only go if it is an organised event. Thus several Americans came to the weekly museum cultural event for the first time while I was there. That was only because Bev put out a call that she had organised a bus for the trip. We were introduced to a steel drummer who gave us a variety of jazz, musical and classical renditions. But the most interesting part was when we went up afterwards and got him to explain how he played it. Then some drummers whipped up some trance inducing rhythms. At first I suspected this was a 'put on a show for the white folks' do but a poet/songwriter took it much further than that. Her lyrics were about issues far too uncomfortable than for pleasing the tourists.

Over the week I settled into Caribbean time. It began to take all day just to... well I'm not sure; the day just seemed to disappear. I went out with the Hash House Harriers, up in the rain forest, running amongst the rivers, the mud, and the waterfall I'd wanted to visit; and through a village where we got calls of "hassle, hassle." As I was walking at the time we called back "easy, easy." They laughed from their veranda and their beers. After two hours of splashing around in the fast approaching dark I found my way back to the bar. This was a wooden shack, a fridge and two people to serve and take money. It was very simple and very fast; they only sold beer. Around the back two others set up a cooking facility: two large pans and a tall pot on gas burners. Here they served 'Oldown,' the national dish of Grenada with crayfish soup. The seventy or so hashers were soon happy, drinking beer and eating while they swopped hashing stories. Then, just as the announcements were starting, the massive music system went into action and drowned them out. We left at that point as our driver, a Bajun studying at St Georges University, had to go but I was impressed by the way in which a complete facility had been erected so successfully on a country road.

Mike and Bev left to do another yacht charter. I took them out for a meal to say thanks but they wouldn't let me pay for it.

I felt a bit disoriented; they had been my anchor in Prickly Bay. It reminded me that I too would soon be moving on. I too had started to put down roots there. All this trip I had been concerned with getting to this Bay and meeting them. With no UK friends having made a definite plan to meet me over here I was faced with moving on, to hopefully make new friends along the way. But it seemed an episode was over.

Cruising has been defined as long periods of time at anchor, with occasional long sails in between. I had slowly delayed the 'moving on' while I got around to getting gas, water and fuel for the boat. But, finally, I decided it was time to go when I noticed weed growing on the anchor chain. I said goodbye to Prickly Bay and sailed past St Georges up the west coast of Grenada towards Carriacou. I wasn't so much making a long passage but a week or so of day sails. I managed to get the start timing all wrong; it was getting dark as I rounded the north of the Grenada, so I altered course for a little town of Sauters. This turned out to be not so much an anchorage but a shallow piece of water between a set of rocks and a beach with breaking waves all around. I was not going in there. Back to Plan A. Having lost an hour or two, I set off for Carriacou again. On the way I sailed over a sometimes active volcano called Kicking Jenny. There is supposed to be an exclusion zone around it but no one takes any notice. I had to sail over it just to say I'd done it. I got to Tyrrel Bay just after midnight. I'd been sleeping for twenty minute sessions in the choppy seas. All I could see in the bay were a few anchor lights and a hulk at anchor. As I got closer I could see more anchor lights and more things I could not identify. The darkness and tiredness seemed to add layers of imagination on to what I could see. I picked the first space I could see and dropped the anchor. Then I sat awake for an hour checking that it was holding. I didn't want to wake up drifting on to a reef. Finally, I got a good night's sleep.

Tyrrel Bay turned out to have a ribbon village along the

shore where every building had turned its attention towards the visiting yachts. There was nothing to see so I went for a walk out along a road towards the end of the island. Here there were large, expensive looking houses. I felt watched as I picked my way through the, now, unmetaled road and down to the shore. It reminded me of a programme I'd seen about lottery winners years ago. One winner had bought a very large house. When his friends came to visit they still sat in the kitchen and slugged beer out of cans, even though they had plenty of other rooms now. Here, there was loud music coming from the large balconies just the same as downtown in the shacks. But it didn't seem as friendly with the high fences and driveways. Walking the other way I bumped into an English couple. At first I thought they were cruisers but they were on their umpteenth shore holiday in the islands. They'd been for a long walk across the hills and were on their way back for a swim before tea. Not bad for several years into their retirement. They seemed to specialise in finding cheap accommodation over here. This time they were in the next town north; where I needed to go to clear customs.

I ate out that night; somehow I had lost the drive to cook. The next day my lethargy had got worse. It took me nearly three hours to get enough motivation to weigh anchor to go to beautiful little island with a sandy beach and good snorkeling. I beached the dinghy and spent all of ten minutes in the sea before going back to the boat. I upped anchor and moved to anchor in Hillsborough. Here I went ashore to have a beer with the couple from the day before. It was fun seeing them but I got back to the boat with an aching skin. I slept fitfully, and with a headache. It was some while later that I realised that I must have a minor virus.

As I cleared out of customs the next morning I got told off by the immigration man for not saying "good morning." "In these islands we say good morning" he said with clear meaning. A Norwegian couple and I stood silently, like kids in front of the head teacher. As he'd been dealing with another yottie I thought this a bit off; to interrupt them would have been rude. I kept these thoughts to myself lest I upset him more. Across the road, I was celebrating successful processing by having a coffee when I noticed the Swedish boat from La Coruna and Las Palmas. We met for a ginger beer. We swapped stories of the crossing and places we liked. They had arrived at Barbados and going south before heading for Panama so we were not going to meet again. They had taken thirty three days crossing. Kirsten said that seeing the land was finally a confirmation that they were actually moving. After all that time with no change in the sea she felt that they must be sitting still. In chatting with them I realised that I'd been missing the community feel of cruisers. I'd been pretty much on my own for the last few days; or amongst charter boats. They tend to be quite insular on their week or fortnight holiday. That made me feel glad that for all the times, over the years when I've been chartering on sailing holidays, that I have gone and chatted to cruising boats.

I sailed on to Clifton on Union Island. It was the same there, lonely, mainly charters, and a few cruisers. The local businesses were based around sailing. But it was colourful and friendly. I couldn't be bothered to cook so I ate cheese sandwiches and watched a film.

I woke feeling much better. Ashore I found good coffee and walked up to the old fort. This had a 280 degree panoramic view over Carriacou, Palm Island and over the Tobago Cays. In the sun they looked beautiful; the horseshoe reef was clear in the coral and the nest of masts at anchor sat above copper blue water. I sat up there for a long time just letting my thoughts wander. It was a bit like being at sea. I could have a thought and then just let it drift away. That night I had a shower in the local hotel. It was a disappointment. I was expecting some form of semi-luxury; it turned out to be a concrete room in the toilet block. The water heater didn't work and the drain was blocked.

I had a couple of beers before returning to the boat.

The lethargy returned again. I didn't even leave the boat the next day. I was woken from one of the many snoozes by Christina and Andreas, a Swedish couple on Nada, calling by. Almost immediately, Asaf and Liat, an Israeli couple on Jinja appeared. We had a good chat about our very similar experiences with the sea and weather getting here. Jinja was off north to pick up Asaf's mother and Nada was heading back south for some diving. Even though they were off again it picked me up to see them. As it was very windy the next day I stayed in Clifton. I spent my time on practical and domestic maintenance.

I sailed to the Tobago Cays. All that is said about them is true. They are beautiful; three little islands surrounded on three sides by a horseshoe reef. The approach is a bit tricky but navigation is eased by the clear sea and the bright sandy bottom. It is now a marine park with protection for the turtles and other wildlife; but it is overrun by charter boats. It seemed like hundreds of charter catamarans and a few monohulls were anchored in every available inch. Dinghies whizzed by taking their crews to the reef and back; while the boat boys plied their wares, barbecues, lobsters, bread etc, in their full speed wooden boats. And then the parties started. I saw one boat realise that it was going to be kept awake by their neighbours; it rapidly moved off to anchor elsewhere.

Just after anchoring I noticed the boat beginning to roll. The tide had risen enough for the wind, which had not died below strong for days now, to blow the swell over the reef. This was repeated every tide. I stayed there for two days, finally giving up after having had only one, half-hour, snorkeling attempt. A friend told me that, in her travels, the things she'd looked forward to often turned out to be the most disappointing, while unplanned things provided the most joy. I had imagined visiting the Tobago Cays for years; now here I was unable to enjoy them.

The next island up is Canouan. This island has tried to become a sort of Mustique, an exclusive island. The Raffles Group have turned half of it into an exclusive resort. Charleston Bay, where I anchored, is largely fronted by a low hotel. I carried out my usual procedure of digging the anchor in and testing it before going ashore. When I returned I noticed that I was close to the yacht Alidorro. I didn't know them but I had heard their radio traffic all the way up from Grenada. One morning, on the cruisers' net, they had put out a warning about their experience with potential piracy on the way up from Trinidad. Outside Carriacou their mainsail had ripped; and off Union Island their engine had failed. I went over to say hello and was immediately offered a beer. We chatted about their adventures and experiences. At first I thought that they were a skippered, charter outfit as they had what looked like a young couple and an older couple plus another single woman on board. Conscious that I didn't want to hold up their supper preparations I left to make my own. I had only been back a few minutes when they called and invited me to eat with them.

I learned that the young couple were cousins, their son and niece; the older couple were her best friend from school, in Trinidad, and husband; and the other woman was an ex-work colleague, now friend. We had a tasty soup and drank the bottle of wine I'd brought from Portugal. They lived four months a year on the boat in the Caribbean and the rest in Norfolk, very close to where I used to live. I didn't remember the steam engine museum that they'd developed though.

I was thinking that I would leave soon when the rain came, and with it, a fantastic squall. My dinghy, moored alongside, jumped and bucked, trying to lose its painter. Rowan suggested that I leave it a while as it was likely that I would have capsized in that wind. Most of us moved below but I stayed up to watch while Hannah, the niece, stayed up to avoid sea sickness. I asked her about herself. She was a dancer. In slow stages, though talk of salsa dancing and Strictly Come Dancing, I found out that she was a West End star and has worked with the best. I Googled her later: she was the lead, "Baby," in the musical version of Dirty Dancing.

In the dark it was difficult to make out where my boat was. We got out a powerful torch but, even with playing it up and down the line of anchored boats for a while, it was difficult to make her out. It was still too windy to go back and, anyway, my dinghy was now upside down under the stern of Alidorro with the outboard under water. I slept on deck. With seven of them they filled the cabins and the seats in the saloon. Sleep was difficult with the frequent gusts of wind and the accompanying rain. The sprayhood or the bimini would flap with a great crack, the wind would howl through the lines while the wind generator would scream. The boat would heel and I would have to hold on. In broken spells I had mumbled sleep until just before daylight, I thought I heard voices. Having imagined several other things during the night I didn't believe me. Then I realised that the voices were in German and I don't imagine in German! I looked up ahead to see a catamaran drifting down towards our bow. I jumped up, banged on the companionway and shouted for "all hands" while running up to the bow. Just as I got there the cat got control and motored away. In three seconds I had woken the whole boat and now they weren't needed. No one blamed me but I did feel a bit embarrassed.

Some went back to bed while the rest of us had tea or coffee. As the dawn broke through I saw Safe Arrival. She was about 200 metres away from where I had left her. Rowan and I got my dinghy out of the way, lowered theirs and drove across. It was obvious that someone had been aboard to stop her dragging further. The charter cat in front was directly over her anchor chain so we called to them. They explained that she had gently bumped into them; that they had let out more chain and then tied her to them. The night watchman appeared and, together, we moved her away and on to a mooring. It was a nice feeling as well in that, not only could I now relax, this was the first time since Lanzarote where I had someone else on board to take control of one end of the boat. It was just so much simpler.

We sorted out my dinghy, had pancakes for breakfast and both boats set sail for Bequia. It was a lively sail upwind and in choppy seas. I arrived just before dark having been soaked several times in the day; from spray coming over the bows and, with the wind, spitting like hail; and from the squalls. The wind held a sustained thirty two knots for five minutes in some of these. I picked a spot amongst the hundreds of boats in Admiralty Bay, dug the anchor in and slept well that night.

Rowan woke me early to take my outboard in for a service. He knew a place that would do it. Once it was delivered, I wandered the town, took in the internet and had a coffee. I met a couple from Prickly Bay and had a chat. I met one of the Trinidadians and we had another coffee. Then the Israelis came by. They'd seen me anchor and had been calling me all morning; and then the son and niece came by. Assaf and Liat talked us into going off for a walk to a nearby bay. It was nice to wander the roads in the shade and chat. Chatting while walking is stimulating and relaxing at the same time; the changing environment stimulates new topics while the familiar movement is comforting.

We took longer than expected so I missed picking up my outboard from the mechanic. We met some others (another Israeli couple and a Franco-Oz couple) for sundowners in a bar and, later, had a meal. One of them looked like the actor, Richard Kitchen, who plays a disillusioned policeman at the start of WWII. Not to be caught out again I asked him if he was famous. "Yes" he replied and they all laughed. No, he wasn't. They invited me to join them on a nature hike up in the rainforests of St Vincent the next day. As St Vincent has the reputation of less lawfulness than the other islands, and it is not recommended to walk alone, I accepted the invite.

I was picked up a six o'clock; another early morning. We caught the ferry over and a reggae bus up to the mountains. From there we walked up steep hills to the nature reserve; then we were on a track that wound through and over the hills and along a fast river. The Satany tree has routes a bit like harbour walls. Great, thin slices of root form buttresses several feet away from the trunk. Assaf scrambled up on and then grabbed a hanging creeper to make a Tarzan swing back to the ground. There was a section for parrot watching. We didn't see any but we could hear their great screeches scratching through our ears.

Later we did see some parrots but these were in captivity. On the way back we visited the Botanical Gardens. Anthony, our guide, had been brought up working with spices in the garden so he could talk about anything there. He picked lemon grass from under our feet, he snuck mace/nutmeg from a tree, he picked a cinnamon bark and he found coriander leaves. All these he would crumple and rub on our palms. Towards the end I was olfactorally overwhelmed; but the smells were good. And then we visited the parrots – they were not screeching this time. He explained that they didn't breed in captivity so they were there as part of a programme to get them back to the wild; a kind of Born Free.

When I first arrived in Grenada I found the patois a foreign language, largely incomprehensible, but over the weeks I have found it almost easy to understand. Going to a very mixed school I think I must have picked up a lot more than I knew. I was lying back listening when I realised this. Anthony started introducing some patois and Rastafarian bits into his talk as he relaxed. He prompted lots of questions which I knew the answers to, particularly about Rastafarianism. After that I listened to the locals more carefully; perhaps I could get the gist better than I thought. In the month I've been here it is becoming clearer. Over the following weeks I have several times been sitting alone when people have been talking about me. If I smiled or looked up when they made a comment about me they have been quite surprised: "You know wha' I say?"

We had a good lunch in the capital, Kingstown, and got back to Bequia. At the quayside we said goodbye. Out of the four boats two were going south the next day and one north. I was staying here. We make friends easily at sea but we can lose them quickly too; they fade into stories of "oh yes, they are in the Gambia" or other such places when we meet new friends who know them too. And, like my outboard, the next day, we may meet them again along the way.

11 STORIES

Looking back on this trip I have become aware of distinct phases. Initially I was adapting to the changes in lifestyle; the launderette, the small living space and the new time frame. After that I had a period where I wasn't sure if I could continue. I think this was where I came to terms with the size of the journey. Once I'd joined the cruisers' routes I became part of a cruising community. Lately though, I have realised another part of what makes the trip so good: it's the stories that people bring to the table. There are so many to remember: Mike and Bev, in Grenada, from Bristol, Liat and Assaf from Israel, Jim, on a boat called "Bobby Dazzler," from Nottingham, Anthony, our guide in the St Vincent Botanical Gardens, Mas, sailing and paddling around the Scandinavian extremities, Charlie Brown, our taxi driver on a tour around St Lucia. All these people have had interesting lives, very different to the standard-ish lives that I'm used to in Bristol.

Charlie Brown told me about his days as a "cop" in St Lucia. I had to press him to talk and he wouldn't be specific; there seems to be a convention to keep the nastier sides of island life away from the tourists. And, as cruisers, we are definitely doing the tour. But the conversation allowed me to get a feel for the island and how he had grown up. Having never left the Caribbean, and even as a taxi driver, the idea of a long drive was very different from those of the mixed nationalities he had in the taxi that day. We had English, Finnish, Faroese, Spanish and Norwegians all asking him questions from our different perspectives. The one thing we all agreed on, however, was that we weren't going to spend forty US dollars in the, vanishing horizon swimming pooled, high on the cliff, beautiful views, expensive, lunch stop of his choice. We went back to a small town and had rotis on the seafront.

I had stayed in Bequia for over a week. In that time I began to scratch beneath the surface of the 'yottie' facing town. One woman I got chatting to was staying in a hostel. In exchange for reduced rent she was using her creative writing teaching skills to help the owner draft his book. She told me one of his stories when he had tackled a burglar with a knife in his house; the burglar had been injured and now the owner was considered "hard." But he was still traumatised by it.

One day I cycled around the island. I met a young lad who showed me his patch, the leafy suburb area near the top of the hill. It was beautiful; the gardens were tended with lots of imagination. It was also clear, though, that there were wire fences around every one and barking, guard dogs all over. In another part I came across the seedier side; later, I learnt that there is a small crack problem. Funnily, they all wanted to buy my tiny, rusty, squeaking, folding bike that I'd swapped for a bottle of rum in Grenada. I couldn't see why they would want it, the roads were steep and full of potholes and the bike was in poor condition.

In complete contrast I met a woman working as a chef on a superyacht. The owners were hardly ever there and even when they were they don't actually take any part in the sailing of it. It seemed that they were trying to break into the Mustique set. To do this they had to invest in the island and show their wealth by sailing there every now and then; a sort of millionaire version of keeping up with the Jones. So all she had to do was to sit around eating cake and reading in nice surroundings with the occasional meal to cook and the odd bit of sailing.

On the dinghy dock the next day I heard her call:"Hi Mr Bristol" (we hadn't exchanged names, just our stories on how we'd got there – a graduate of Bristol University, she had gone into hospitality and been running a ranch in Africa where some guests had asked to work on their yacht in the Caribbean.) She was inviting me to a goodbye drink; she had to leave the next day for family reasons. I couldn't go as Mike and Bev had just arrived on Whitebird and had invited me across for the evening. It was lovely to see them and catch up on news; they'd broken their charter jinx and finally had some guests who enjoyed being on a boat. As I left them that night the sky opened like the sluice gates at Bristol docks. Within seconds I was totally drenched. I couldn't see anything. The rain sped like bullets past my head torch beam and stung where they hit me. I was disoriented. Suddenly, I recognised the bow of Safe Arrival. I was home; and then the rain stopped.

I had a hard sail out of Bequia. I opted to pass along the East side of St Vincent toward St Lucia. Although it made it easier to reach the island on one tack it meant facing the untamed waves from the Atlantic. I pitched and rolled in the choppy sea for eleven hours before making it into a small harbour by the airport at the south of St Lucia. The flashing green light that I relied on to find my spot stopped working just as I dropped my anchor; the lights in the West Indies are notoriously unreliable. Two large motor cruisers stopped off near me. As I left the next morning I heard some planes land in the local airport. A short while later these boats sent dinghies ashore and, a while later, they overtook me on the way around the island. I suppose they were picking up their owners or guests.

I caught my second fish, a Spanish Mackerel. It was a perfect size for two good meals. I had a nice lunch as I motor sailed around to Rodney Bay. Rodney Bay is where the ARC make landfall from Las Palmas. By European standards it is big but, for the Caribbean it is enormous. In the middle of the bay there is a small canal that leads into a hidden lagoon with space for yachts, superyachts and an anchorage. It made me think of kids' adventure stories about hidden moorings. As I came in I heard Gaia, the Faroes boat on the radio and called them back. Within an hour of tying up I had had my first proper shower in over two months, and was waiting for them in a bar on the dockside.

There I met Liat and Assaf plus the others from the day out in St Vincent. Within ten minutes Liat had convinced me to take part in the next day's 'round the island' race. I would be crewing on Avocette, a Pacific Seacraft, one of the boats I dream about owning.

All of us were going to Jump Up Friday, a nearby village fair. It is like a carnival but is small and almost entirely concerned with food. A short section of street is shut off while street vendors sell whatever they can, mainly food. There is a sound system at the end playing mostly Bob Marley. I have noticed a dearth of live bands in this part of the world. Most of the ones I have seen have been European in origin. I wondered why this was; is it the poverty? And yet other poor countries manage to produce musicians. I remembered that in Cuba the musicians would often start playing Buena Vista Social Club tracks when tourists were present. Is Bob Marley played because most tourists wouldn't identify with any other reggae?

After a scramble through customs and immigration, the next morning I joined my team on Avocette and we set off for the start line. Racing fever returned for the first time in years as we set up pole position and then wasted it. The first two hours were great as we all jockeyed for position; but then the winds died off and we all drifted in the tide around the rocky headlands. With a five hour motor and arrival in the dark, or a two hour motor back we voted to return. We then picked up our own local wind and had a boisterous sail back. The ones who continued did not get this on the other side of the island. They all gave up and motored to the finish.

Liat and Assaf sped off by bus to join the others at the midpoint while Chris, the owner, and I got drunk like Brits do. Somewhere during our demise into unconsciousness we bumped into Gaia who invited us on their taxi tour of the island the next day. So, nursing a two brufen hangover, I joined this multinational tour of St Lucia. We were first shown the education centre. This is in the ex-British barracks; it felt like we were being taken to prison. And then Charlie Brown kicked in with his commentary. We had a fascinating tour of Soufriere, Castries and the Pietons, with their volcanic sulphur baths. They stank of sulphur but the guide said this was good; if the concentration grows to lethal levels then it becomes odourless. I also learnt that the island has produced two Nobel Prize winners, neither of whom I had heard of. We also saw the damage from Hurricane Thomas, last October. He had grown from a depression into a Grade II hurricane in two hours. It was not the wind but the following rain that had done most of the damage. Great swathes of earth showed where the hills had let go; everything in these strips had slid off into the valleys; houses, roads, trees. And already small layers of green had started to regrow.

After going to meet the more determined racers at the prize giving in the yacht club Chris and I went back to the marina to finish the evening with our tour party. This was the last night in Rodney Bay for most of them. Late at night Randi arrived from Colombia where she had been kite surfing. Since I last saw her in Las Palmas she had been in fifteen different countries around Europe and the Caribbean. And the next day she was off in Gaia towards Tobago for the carnival.

I stayed for over a week in Rodney Bay. Rodney was an admiral in the days of wars between the UK and France. A lot of the places in the Caribbean seem to be named after naval commanders who fought here. I spent a fair bit of time with Chris, the owner of the yacht we'd raced in. He seemed, at first, to be a salty dog. He obviously had a lot of sailing experience, had crossed the Atlantic several times before and was a much faster drinker than me. As the week went by I found out that there was a lot more to him. At university he'd managed to get elected to the student union. Part of his job was to get a new bar built. The competition to supply the bar from the breweries was such that one had entertained him and some friends to a Miss World lunch. I could imagine the hormones of three young males as he told me. Later, he had started a windsurf board business with a friend. On a more serious note he had taught maths and water sports to kids with learning difficulties. It was another lesson to me not to judge books by their covers. I could easily have been put off by my initial impression that he was a right wing, conventional sailor. I learned all this one day when we walked around the northern end of the island. We got slightly lost amid the expensive, architect designed houses and their leafy drives. There were some savage looking dogs too. But we persevered to find our way to the Easterly beaches and look at the Atlantic waves crashing in.

One evening he helped me move out of the marina to refuel and then to anchor before he had to get to another appointment. I went to pick up some money owing to us but my outboard ran out of fuel. I was rowing back, against the wind, when I heard a shout. He and a couple of others were having sundowners on a new boat in town. I rowed back to give him his money when the owner asked if 'the postman' wanted a beer. Never one to refuse hospitality I went aboard where I discovered who Chris' appointment was. He had taken Terry sailing in the Solent a few years ago. She had loved it so much that she became a semi-professional crew. We were now guests of her present employer, David, who came from Norfolk. We talked nonsense in the Norfolk dialect for a few minutes while we found out that they knew my old haunts. He and his wife had his cousin over on holiday and they were expecting another crew to arrive the next day. I wondered what were the pitfalls of employing strangers on boats while travelling from country to country. David's cousin, Cat, was staying for three weeks. While in conversation I found out that she used to skydive at Langar, near Nottingham. If she had continued for one more year I would have known her from there. It does seem a small world sometimes. She had given up skydiving for sailing and scuba. In the way that sometimes happens, we established a connection in the brief time I was on the boat. We stayed in email contact for the rest of the year while I was travelling but I have not seen her since that night.

Also on board were Phil and Danielle, one of the couples I'd been to St Vincent with. They met in 1975 when Phil, an Ozzie, had been in France. After a year he had had to return to Oz but promised he would return. Daniele had realised that a year was too long for separation so had turned up at his door a few weeks later. Thirty six years on they were sailing around the world together. They had won the round the island race. It turns out that this was not surprising as Danielle had been Junior 420 European champion.

Asaf and Liat had joined them on the second day of the race. This young Israeli couple backpacked around South America a few years ago. There it had occurred to them to see if they could get back to Europe by crewing on a boat. Unfortunately, they had chosen to crew with either an incompetent or unlucky skipper. He had taken them into a storm just west of the Azores. They had been unable to stop at any but the most Easterly island after twenty four hours of fifty five knot winds. Undeterred, they bought a yacht when they got home, did it up, and were now on their own North Atlantic circuit. They put me to shame with the energy they had, putting up new bits of equipment, sailing back and forth around the islands and diving wherever they were. They had come on the race to learn from us. Apart from a few racing rules I couldn't find anything to teach them; they were avid learners and were good at putting it into practice.

Jim was another solo sailor, from Nottingham but his boat was usually moored in Dartmouth. He had a thirty two foot boat as well. The difference was that his was laid out as a yawl with a mast right at the back of the boat. He had a large cockpit space, much more comfortable than mine, but down below he was cramped. On the crossing he had slept on the floor. Also, on the way, he had discovered that his mizzen sail interfered with his wind pilot so he couldn't use it. The usual way of reefing a yawl is simply to take down the mainsail. That's why his didn't have any reefing points in the main. Because he had to take down the mizzen he now had no way of reefing bar rolling up the genoa or taking the main down completely. So his sail settings were an unbalanced all or nothing. His main sail was currently in the sailmakers, having reefing points sewn in.

It was easy to stay in Rodney Bay. I was anchored in the lagoon, quiet and flat, with friends around and good support services. But we were all waiting for a change in the weather. It is supposed to blow fifteen knots from the East out here in the spring; for almost all the time I had been there it has blown more than twenty knots from the North East. That has meant a hard slog to windward ever since Grenada. I wondered if the sailing will ever get back to the easy Atlantic crossing level that I had got used to.

12 MARTINIQUE TO GUADELOUPE

The winds kept up their twenty five knots from the North East. I was fed up; Rodney Bay was nice but I'd been there enough time. I wanted to move on. So, casting my lot to the weather I made a passage to Martinique. It meant crashing through the high waves and getting covered in sea water time and time again and, with the wind in the wrong direction, it meant tacking so adding half as much distance again. The then squalls got up. The wind switched by thirty degrees in these mini cyclones. I had no chance of reaching Le Marin on the south coast without putting the engine on. Eventually, I got into the lee of the headland where the sea was calmer and I could go at a good speed into the Cul de Sac du Marin. It is an enormous bay but, like Poole, with islands and shallows all over. It was getting dark as I arrived but, fortunately, the French islands are considered to be part of France and keep their navigation lights to EU standards. And then, just as I was dropping anchor, another squall came in. Visibility was down to a few feet. I had to peer very hard to see anything; checking the anchor for dragging was now down to feel on the chain rather than any visual clues. There were boats all around and I didn't want to rev the engine high in case the anchor did drag and I careered backwards into one of them.

If Rodney Bay marina was European then Le Marin marina was up another level. I went ashore. Everything was just like the marinas in France. There were chandleries and NavAid equipment stores, charter companies and brokers all along the front. And there was a cafe which, apart from the name, would have sat comfortably in a Brittany sea front. The customs formalities were carried out on a PC with only sensible questions to answer. They didn't want to know the make of my radar (always a difficult one as I don't have radar.) I was back at the beginning of my journey. Back in Euro-land; and back to expensive coffee.

I wanted to buy a GPS to plug into my laptop. I'd been trying to buy one since Grenada but to no avail. I asked here. "Which type would you prefer?" he asked. I was befuddled for a second. Firstly, by his response and secondly because Asaf and Liat had walked in at that moment; they were impressed that I could speak French. It's only the second time that I have impressed anyone with my language skills since I started. The moment was ruined by my pause as he transferred to English. But at least I could now turn on my laptop, plug in a couple of USB things and be able to 'see' ships on the chart. It meant that I will have better vision, and will know the names of the ships about to run me down, when the inevitable fog closes in on the Western approaches to the English channel.

I said goodbye to Asaf and Liat. They may not be able to visit Antigua as they need visas. Asaf's mother was originally going to meet them in St Vincent but couldn't because the flight went through Antigua. She had been making enquiries back in Israel for them while sorting out to meet them that night in Martinique. I sailed on to Fort du France, the capital. That was a lovely sail. I can't remember the last time I could say that except for the crossing. I anchored right up against the Fort. If they had wanted to throw stones at me they could have struck me easily. It was so close that I didn't bother with the outboard engine. I just rowed ashore.

Further up the coast in St Pierre, a few days later, I had an unhappy thought. This was the third stop in Martinique; they had all been very different. I had wandered inland in Le Marin to find it a sleepy little town much like when Mark and I wandered up from L'Aber Wrac'h. Here I had chatted, badly in French, in the supermarket. In Fort du France I had wandered around the, slightly industrialised, city looking for a launderette. In St Pierre I hiked up into the hills above the town. I realised that since arriving on this island I have not been greeted by anyone. All the friendly questions from total strangers, all the banter and help was missing. Le Marin marina was white, the town was black. St Pierre was black apart from the holiday makers. When meeting in the street I noticed that I wasn't looked in the eye until I initiated conversation. Was this a facet of a more sophisticated society? Was it a French version of racism? It wasn't overt; was it that I have been out of Europe for some time and got used to a different culture. Do I behave like this in Europe?

St Pierre is almost Creole. A small town it was completely wiped out in 1902 when the local volcano exploded over it. Owing to elections and political influences no one was evacuated; the result was that everyone bar one man in his cellar and a prisoner in a dungeon were killed. Some of the ruins are still visible. While I was there they had their own little carnival. Some of us yotties went ashore. We were practically the only visitors there. The locals wore the most electric of colours. Fluorescent greens, pinks, oranges were used in t-shirts, short pants, tights, bras and head scarves. Netting seemed to be the theme as virtually every other person had either a netting t-shirt or tights; male and female. Boots and fluorescent leg warmers also seemed to be order of the day. It was mesmerising. By nine o'clock I'd eaten and drunken enough; and listened to enough loud music, some live, to make me drowsy. I rowed back to the boat and fell asleep dreaming of the really bad jugglers and to the sound of "Oranges and Lemons" incorporated into a reggae tune.

The hills up by St Pierre are extraordinary. Imagine a crumpled piece of paper laid flat between two hands. Then move the hands together so that the paper creases, mainly in straight lines but also, in some curved and angles too. I walked up a valley with near vertical sides. As the road curved around near the top I turned off towards the steam-driven rum distillery. High on the island it sits surrounded by sugar cane fields and a sewage plant. It was closed to visitors on Sundays but the restaurant was open. I had a coffee and wandered around anyway. I read a trashy adventure story for a while and wandered back. Looking around I tried different routes back. I had walked only a few hundred metres along one side road when it turned abruptly. I was now on the edge of a different valley. I looked down a couple of hundred feet below me to another river running fast through rocks. Up I could see the valley twisting like when I used to decorate the icing on cakes when I was a kid. I'd take a fork and run it through the icing and lift little peaks with the flat of a knife. The next road was a contour, serpentine along the edge of the near vertical hill. In each of these valleys the greenery reminded me of something; it took me a long while to realise that these were wild, and very big, versions of my pot plants at home.

I had to stay an extra night in St Pierre. The customs computer is in a restaurant which was closed for the carnival. But I couldn't be bothered to stay any longer after that so I left without checking out. I wasn't worried as I still had my checking out papers form St Lucia.

The carnival, The Mardi Gras, had started for me in St Pierre. I didn't see the it in Roseau, my first stop there in Dominica, but I certainly heard it. I had only overnighted on a yellow flag before heading on to Portsmouth, as, back in Martinique, I had responded to a request by some crew. I was going to meet the two of them in Portsmouth, Dominica. Also, I had been recommended to take the Indian River trip there.

Beth and Kelly had been staying in Portsmouth for two weeks. They had been crewing on another boat but had fallen out with the owner. She had tried to dictate their lives to what and when they could eat; where they could go; and if they could close their own cabin doors. She had only told them, once they arrived, that they were not sailing anywhere for three weeks.

Then she had formed an alliance with a man who seemed to treat them like slaves. That was too much for them so they had left. I was now introduced to the bureaucracy of changing crew when abroad. I had to visit both customs and immigration with their previous skipper to transfer them onto my crew list.

It turned out that Beth was from Bristol; less than 300 metres from my house. She was competent crew. Kelly was an experienced sailor from Cornwall. They had formed a strong friendship by looking after each other both on board and in Dominica. The presence of two English women staying in a house on their own had given them a certain amount of notoriety. They had a 'not past the gate' policy for all the interested Dominican men – and there were several. When I arrived, the first boat boy, Alexis, to come out to me, had asked if I was "the guy taking the two women." I finished the carnival with them there that night. It consisted of a truck with a band on it going around the square. Each song lasted about half an hour and they only seemed to have four songs. There was a crowd who would mosey along in front of the truck and a bigger crowd behind. Every woman seemed to have a man shimmying along behind her as they reggae-danced along.

The next morning I was picked up by Alexis and taken, my head thundering from the Step Ups, (a ginger wine in a glass of rum) to the Indian River. This is a national park, full of birds and fauna. I saw three different types of heron, osprey, all sorts of trees and birds of paradise. Any pot plants I hadn't seen in St Pierre were here too. I saw an elephant ivy. When I had first got together with a girlfriend, thirty years before, she had bought a tiny, two leafed plant in the local shop. Twelve years later we had to get rid of it because it had grown over ten feet tall. I loved that plant. It was a massive philodendron with large, split leaves. And here it was, looking small in the wild but very much bigger than the one we had given away. That made my day.

We were constrained by money for the next few days. The

cashpoint in Portsmouth was out of cash. Kelly lent me some money to be going on with to be paid back in Les Saintes. Unfortunately, the cashpoint there had also run out of cash. It had been a lively sail across there and we were looking forward to some coffee, cheese and other accoutrements of French fare. For Beth and Kelly this was a massive culture shock. They had got so used to the enforced chicken diet and search for food on Dominica that they had difficulty taking it all in. It was very pretty there. A group of small islands, like Scilly only taller, were never developed agriculturally so there was never any slavery. They are now a holiday destination, crowded out with restaurants and mopeds, for the reasonably well off French – a gourmandise explosion for Beth and Kelly. We had to pick where we could eat or buy food by the presence of a card reader. Not all the cafes took plastic and it would have been uncomfortable, if not interesting, to have been unable to pay.

We saved our last Euros to see the fort. It has an interesting museum but, by far, the best things about it are the views; and the enormous iguanas. As we walked around the walls we could see through the islands to Dominica in the south, Marie Galante to the east and Guadeloupe to the north. It was wonderful to get a different perspective on the distances and directions that I have been travelling.

In the afternoon we set off for Guadeloupe. It was supposed to be only ten miles away. That is correct if just going to the south coast; but we were going to the middle of the island isthmus, fifteen miles further on. We didn't arrive until way after dark, into a complicated entrance lit by thousands of buoys all flashing their own tune. It was like the Solent but without so many vessels. Beth was a keen competent crew and Kelly a fine sailor; that made it a lot easier. Just before dark we caught a barracuda. We were looking forward to a fish supper but when we worked out how heavy it was we threw it back. Barry the barracuda was over two kilos; at this weight he was a likely source of citaguella poisoning. Citaguella can cause neurological problems so it is not to be trifled with. But we did take a picture of him.

The marina in Guadeloupe, Pointe a Pitre, was fairly uninteresting. Apart from having to find the longest rope so that we could tie the stern to a buoy thirty metres away from the pontoon it could have been anywhere. We wandered out to look at the town and found that we were effectively on the edge of a sort of retail trading estate for bars and restaurants. Beyond that there was practically nothing. We had to walk for half an hour to get into town. The architecture here was largely Creole so that made up a bit for the walk. But, as it was Sunday, nothing was open. We walked back to the boat and tried the showers. They were new, cold and dirty. I felt embarrassed for having brought Beth and Kelly to this place. I'm sure it would have been better if it had been open. For our time there we relied on ourselves. Kelly and I went to the aquarium which was very good. We discovered that the citiguella poison risk area is to the north of Guadeloupe so we could have eaten Barry Barracuda.

There was one tank with some sharks in. The white ones swam continuously, gliding around with their fins sometimes above the surface. They seemed to move effortlessly. Just every now and then would they flick their fins and accelerate across the tank in an instant. It made me realise how dangerous they would be in the open sea. I wouldn't stand a chance at getting away. In complete contrast there were several nurse sharks who lay on the floor of the tank and didn't move the whole time we were there.

We left the marina at four in the morning. There is a canal running through the middle of Guadeloupe. They only open the bridges over it in the early hours so we had to be at the first one at five o'clock, ready to catch the second at twenty past. The channel up to the bridge is well lit but we still felt a little excited as we motored through water only a metre below the keel. Suddenly this reduced to twenty centimetres. I tried to pull further into the channel but it reduced further. Something was not right. On the principle that the only known safe water is the place you've just come from, I turned around. The deeper water seemed to be near the red buoy and yet that was telling us to go stay this side of it. After a few minutes of nosing slowly in different directions we realised the mistake. The channel did go the other side of this buoy; it was that this one marked the beginning of a tributary to the left, just where the main channel bends to the left as well. So we were doing the equivalent of turning onto the hard shoulder instead of up the slip road when, really, we wanted to be on the main carriageway.

As we approached the bridge, in the black gloom, it started to lift. We could see a few car headlights stop at the flashing signs and then three yachts came through towards us. We nudged forward around the kink of the river and through into a mangrove swamp. Either side we could see nothing but the dark shapes of trees. The next navigation mark was around a bend so Kelly went forward to look out and I steered down, what I could guess as, the middle of the channel. We were steering by different senses: we could hear the sound of the engine being absorbed by the mangroves on the banks. We could just about feel the damp air surrounding them, with just the occasional whiff of vegetation in the still air. The depth gauge would vary from several metres to practically nothing. Each time it reduced I got slightly worried; there was nothing to help me out here. We would be dependent on the other two yachts travelling through with us. They were bigger and ahead of us so it may have been difficult for them to turn around.

As it dawned, the light showed us the swamps either side. In an almost sepia monochrome, the river opened up in front of us to an enormous bay. There were little islands and reefs all around it. It was beautiful. I was pierced by a feeling of tranquility. As the sun rose the sepia filled out to the bright blues of sea and the green and yellows of the land in classic Caribbean colours. The navigation buoys disappeared in the light. They were too far away to see, even with binoculars and, anyway, we were taking a different route through the reefs towards the North West corner of Guadeloupe. It meant travelling slowly and checking our position regularly as we picked our course around all these dangers. This was what I had imagined navigating in the Caribbean was going to be. I was glad I had the others to help me.

We sailed down to Deshaies around the north west corner of Guadeloupe. Suddenly, the fishing line went taught. We hauled in Barry Barracuda's big brother. We were now definitely in the cituagella danger zone so we needed to let him go. Kelly and I struggled for ages to get the hook out but it was in his tongue way down his throat. Barracudas have a long line of very sharp teeth so we attempted to use tools, a bit like a crash course in dentistry. We failed. We had to kill him and throw him away. I'd taken months to catch two fish and then caught two, both of which we couldn't eat, in two days of sailing.

Deshaies is a pretty little town in a bay. There is a little river which we rowed up to tie to the dinghy dock. In town we met Charlotte from Rusty. Now she was back on Rosa, the Cornish Ketch that she left Falmouth on. She invited us to join them that evening. Jake, her son, remembered painting my face for Halloween. He had taken the long Atlantic crossing of thirty days in his stride without a fuss.

I went for a walk up the river. After a while it turned into a rocky rapid. I climbed up and up, jumping from boulder to boulder and splashing in the pools in between. Suddenly I realised that the sun was going down and I was too far up to get back in daylight. I had no choice but to hurry on to where the road joined the river. In the guide it says this is an hour or two to walk. As the guide might have been written for less active people I guessed that it would be an hour maximum and I had been romping along for some time. I stopped to wash my face and knocked my sunglasses into a pool. They vanished into a whirlpool and, presumably, down into the pool below. That was my second pair lost.

I was not sure if I ever found the road that I was supposed to. I may have passed it in my hurry. Eventually, I found a path off to the side that rose to what looked like it must be a road. It was. I turned down and hurried along past a little cemetery. It seemed out of place on a very steep, wooded hill with the trees hanging over the bright white crosses. I wondered how the grave diggers had managed to dig down six feet while on a steep hill. Or did they dig in horizontally until they were six feet under?

Back on the water I visited Rosa. The inside reminded me of Feit's boat in Gran Canaria. It was not open plan but, because it was so beamy, the saloon was enormous. Eight of us sat around in comfort drinking tea and putting the world to rights. We parted in a bowsprit walking competition. We took it in turns to walk along the pole from the bow to the forestay. Rosa had a bit of a roll on her that night; only one person made it up to the forestay. The rest of us fell off to splash in the dark.

13 ANTIGUA

I'm in my bunk, in the forepeak, contemplating Antigua; this island has been very different from the rest of the places on this trip. The sail here was unremarkable. An early morning start and a close reach took us about ten hours. We entered Falmouth Harbour early evening. Nothing could have prepared us for the sight. This is one of the homes for super yachts; and by super they don't mean fantastic but just very big. These are not really for sailing; they are more for indicating the size of the owners' wallets. The crews seem to spend most of their time polishing the metal work. I motored past the Maltese Falcon (about sixty metres) every time I went ashore. One day there were two crew standing up in their dinghy to polish an anchor, the same size as them. This yacht is unusual in that the masts have no stays. It has curved yard arms and the squarish sails are pulled out from the mast along these arms, top and bottom. The masts are then rotated to catch the wind. It's all made out of what looks like polished plastic.

The crews all get off work around ten o'clock. The bars fill up bright young things who don't seem to have gone abroad. They have re-created their environment in Antigua. I wondered if they would have travelled themselves without the work and accommodation. It seemed to be part of the continuum of travelling. Some people do it by package holiday, some by backpacking, some by gap years and some live it. I think I fitted the third one of those. Connie, the owner of one of the bars, The Mad Mongoose, asked me, rhetorically, why they wanted to drink these shot concoctions when they didn't seem to enjoy them and they were drunk enough already. As she had been running this bar for six years I think she probably knew the answer.

One night the plastic bust came out. It was filled with rum

and carried through the bar; the nipples supplied the rum to whoever sucked on them. It was very popular. It was a scene from a Thomas Pynchon novel I read in my twenties. I never thought that I would ever witness it though. The Swedes I was with that night did their best to get paralytic. It was too easy to drink the rum; it is camouflaged in innocent fruit juices.

On our first night we bumped into Ed and Susie from Betsy. I had met them in Funchal and Grenada. Beth asked Susie if she was enjoying cruising. "No" was her very firm reply. In the following discussion she explained how her experience just didn't come up to the expectations that previous cruisers had led her to. She just didn't understand what they 'got' from the circuit. Beth had similar feelings about Antigua. After two days there she said she just didn't 'get' it. She didn't want to stay any longer and couldn't understand why anyone would. As a globe trotter she had a point. The only thing I could say was that the charter boat crews were working here, the cruisers could rest here before crossing the Atlantic and the race weeks were a big pull.

The customs house was in Nelson's Dockyard in English Harbour, a national park, the renovated buildings of the original English Navy base. It is very well done; the restaurants and shops are all within the red brick and coral stone buildings, similar to the harbour in Grenada. The brick was transported here as ballast; it makes a nice English feel for any homesick person. I was introduced to the complications of transferring crew off a boat. They have to have tickets out, places to stay or another boat to transfer to. As Beth and Kelly didn't have any of these I had to keep them on the crew list. The customs people were very nice about it. They were welcoming and explained it clearly. There was none of the officiousness that I have heard people complain about. We left to consider their next moves. A week later they officially left my crew on a delivery yacht to St Marten.

Shirley Heights, named after another military commander, is an old fort high above the harbours. On Sundays they have a steel band playing up there, followed by a rock/reggae band. I met up with Ian, from The Canaries, in Celtic Spray and we climbed the hundreds of feet up a steep and jagged path to hear the music. It is a tourist point as well. It was interesting to see all the yotties (tanned and lean, bad hair cuts, dressed in faded clothes) in between the tourists (white/pink, good coiffure, ironed clothes.) The steel band played covers of popular songs which built to a crescendo of rhythm. Even having eaten, and in conversation, it was hard not to start moving. The later band were just as good. Ian told me that the bassist was a famous cricketer but didn't know who. I couldn't think until I saw him smile; it was as if his lips were shutters that raised instantly to reveal his white teeth. I remembered that smile every time he dismissed an English batsman. Curtley Ambrose was one of the deadly strikeforce of the great Windies bowling force in the eighties. I felt so much like a kid again that I nearly asked him for his autograph. I didn't. I had a dance instead.

Lots of food, drinks and dances later we staggered to the path. One look at the dark, uneven steepness was enough to convince us that we would walk the road. A van pulled in and offered us a lift. I was glad we accepted as it was several miles back by road. The only trouble was that the driver was going to the same bar as us. That meant that he returned the drinks that we bought him as thanks. After a while I was confused as to who was thanking who. I was confused about getting back to the boat that night. My balance wasn't too good. I decided to lie down on the floor of the dinghy with just my head above the rubber. That way I couldn't fall out. I know it was difficult to heave myself onboard when the boat, the dinghy and the heaver were all rolling about. I don't remember much after that.

One problem I had been wondering about was my stern gland. This is the bearing and seal where the propeller shaft goes through the hull. On the crossing it had leaked and had continued to do so, intermittently, ever since. With help from another cruiser I took the nuts off. It feels silly to undo a nut that holds a seal in place. What if the water gushes in? I'd feel stupid to sink in the harbour. Even after we fixed it I couldn't believe it really works that way: a bit of impregnated rope is wound around the prop shaft and compressed into a tube around the shaft. Then a bit of grease is squeezed onto it. The water outside works its way in through the rope to cool and ease the spin. At the end of the day or at regular intervals, a bit more grease is squeezed in. Did I really cross the Atlantic with this Heath Robinson mechanism?

I was invited to join a party to tour the island in a hire car. We discovered the suburban north, the holiday west, the city of St Johns and the wilder east. We drove up little lanes to see where they went. On one we ignored the sign to keep out unless we worked for Cable and Wireless. A little later the road became a couple of banks with a rocky crevasse in between. Then it got very steep. At this point we agreed that this little car-to-go-shopping-in was probably out of its comfort zone and turned back.

One day I was sitting in Grace B4 Meals, an Antiguan roadside restaurant - a cheap and cheerful, authentic Antiguan food place - when two men sat down near me. I recognised them as the ones who had called out to Chris's (St Lucia) daughters, who were staying with him on Avocette. It turned out that the four had met while flying over from UK. We exchanged stories but something didn't quite fit with theirs. Not that they were lying but it just didn't quite fit. After a few questions from me they realised that I wasn't going to leave it so they took a breath and filled in the rest. The younger man's parents owned Mirabella 3, a forty three metre superyacht. They had problems with the engine and other parts, and also with the crew. It would have made a good case study for a course in teamwork and leadership. The distance between the operating crew and the owners, the culture onboard and the quality of repairs were not good for the morale of a charter ship. It had got to the point where a crew member had complained of having to buy their own toothpaste. Alex, the young one, and Vernon, a family friend, were there to fire fight and get her ready for a crossing to the Mediterranean. I discovered that the skipper gets paid over €100k, tax free with all found on board, plus the use of hire cars and flights home twice a year. I wondered if I might have taken the wrong career path somehow.

I spent many nights sitting in the local bars just observing. I couldn't write theatre like this. One night the crew of Skat, a large motor yacht allegedly owned by one of the top Microsoft executives, were in the Mad Mongoose. This boat is painted battleship grey with black numbers on the side; it looks like a warship. I wondered if the war games idea had just been upped a few million dollar notches. The crew were well into their cups when they gave the landlady, Connie, a crew t-shirt and moved behind the bar to serve whilst drinking. In their crew t-shirts they looked almost professional except they'd donned a selection of wigs and hats found in a cupboard; and for their obvious drunken state. I asked Connie what this was all about; she replied: "It's trash the Mongoose night!" She seemed quite happy about it.

I met Stuart, the owner of a fifty four foot classic yacht Desiderata. He was selling places to crew during classics week. I didn't want to buy one but we got chatting and, being in a bar, one drink led to another until we were well and truly drunk. Somewhere in this time Ian turned up too. The three of us staggered home to our boats at some unearthly hour. The next day, while still hung over but trying to recover by drinking coffee, I met Stuart again. He told me about his sailing history and plans. He'd run a sailing school for physically disabled kids in the Cheshire area. But the lure of the open sea and cruising had been too much for him. He had picked up his boat in Mauritius to sail around the Cape and over to the Caribbean. The plan was to enter all the Classics competitions with paying crew. It seemed to be working.

I went with him to look at his boat. On the way we called in on Mirabella 3. I had gift-wrapped a tube of toothpaste with a note for Alex and Vernon to say that this may help them out with their problems. We drove the dinghy under the stern of this enormous yacht. It occurred to me that I didn't know the protocol for calling on a superyacht. On small yachts you knock on the hull and call the boat name. Someone will usually appear from a hatch to welcome you. But a knock on the hull to this boat would not be heard. Should we go up the tender ladder? I decided to climb up onto the pontoon. It was not so much a pontoon as a concrete road suspended ten feet above the harbour. Just as I was struggling up Alex and Vernon came along. They were interested in Desiderata so Stuart invited them too but first they had some work to complete. They said they'd turn up later.

Desiderata was a relatively recently built boat in GRP; but she was fashioned as an old wooden ketch. She was lovely, lovely lines, quality build and it was a good feeling to sit supping beer in her cockpit. Just as it got dark, we noticed a large dinghy moving slowly around the harbour. It looked like it was looking for something so we watched and, when it came near, hailed it. Yes it was Alex and Vernon, and they were looking for us. We had another tour of the boat and a few more beers. Later, Stuart suggested going ashore for some food. Alex invited us to Mirabella 3 for the leftovers; he and Vernon were working later than the crew so their supper was left out for them. Even then, these leftovers were better quality than some bistros in Bristol.

We had a tour of the boat. The foredeck was massive. The

inside was air conditioned with what can only be described as bedrooms; cabins do not do them justice. There was a lounge and a library and a whole section called crew quarters. We didn't go in there. I explored the service deck. Through a hatch I dropped into this enormous space with thousands of pipes and taps and wires. Hot water tanks stood a many with all the colour coding I could imagine. I have always realised that my boat is a self-sufficient system but it is based on the necessary, removal of unnecessary; and economy. This boat was based on luxury, the means to achieve that, and then the self-sufficiency.

Out on deck again, the clevis pins were as thick as my wrists. We sat at one of the deck tables to eat the supper that we had chosen from the selection and Vernon had zapped in the microwave. Every now and then one of the crew would wander on board or ashore. Life for them would change soon. Once the work was carried out the boat was off to the Med where there were several weeks of charter booked up. At nearly €300k per week the charterees expect perfect service.

Ian finally left Antigua. I was not going to bump into him again. He was going south to avoid the hurricanes and then back up to USA next autumn. He had been nearly three months in Antigua. By then I had been there three weeks. I realised that this was my longest time in one place since Bristol. I had hurried the first part of the Caribbean because I didn't know how long it was going to take to get to Antigua. That, and taking Beth and Kelly onboard, had led to me getting there a couple of weeks earlier than planned. I was staying for the Classics week which meant I was here at least another two weeks. I felt I was slowly being absorbed into Antigua.

In some ways this felt like a downtime. Although I was going out most nights, the growing familiarity of it helped me get my head around the next step. It was not long to the return crossing. My brother might be joining me but that would depend on when I was leaving and where from. One thing I had learnt on this trip was not to say where and when to prospective crew; only either where or when. But I was still undecided about the leaving point. St Martens was 100 miles further on but only shortened the journey by twenty miles. However, it had the best provisioning stores and I could find out about a cruisers' net set up by fellow Transat sailors.

I started to plan a maintenance schedule ready for the return. I lifted the bolts from the back stay chain plate. Every one had started to crevice crack. Although the combined remaining strength of them was greater than the clevis pin that holds the stay it was still worrying. So I inspected all the other chain plate bolts as well. Antigua seemed to have a theme of leaks for me; there was the stern gland now fixed but the water tank and the dinghy both had leaks to be fixed too.

My maintenance was put into the shade by the return of Rosa though. They anchored up one evening and, within a couple of days, had started sanding and repainting the hull, clearing all the decks, repairing rope work and generally turning her in to a respectable entrant for the Classics parade of honour. Then, a couple of days later, Serenity arrived. I introduced Barry and Ann to Stuart and, within, minutes, they were good friends. Borrowing Stuart's dive gear, Barry, an ex-Royal Navy diver, sorted out a way of raising money and awareness for the Men Matters charity. He would scrub boats' bottoms. In the warm waters the weeds had been growing much faster on the hull. The trailing growth can slow a boat down by one knot. Across the Atlantic this would add four days to the crossing. I said I'd have my bottom scraped first. Within hours he had more offers, so many that he had to put mine back a few days; some of these yachts were racing so they had time frames and another was extremely generous to the charity. Meanwhile I fixed my leaks.

During the next week the harbours started filling up with classic yachts. Although there are plenty of real, vintage yachts the emphasis of classics week seemed to be more about the spectacle. Several of the yachts were GRP, some were sloops, some ketches but the main criterion appeared to be that they had a bowsprit. It became quite normal to be amongst white, gleaming, classic lined, multi-masted beauties. The pelicans seemed to be gathering too. I often looked out to see a couple gliding around, scanning the water for signs of fish activity. Then, every now and then, one of them would drop its beak, like an exaggerated Concorde, to dive at high speed into the water. I sometimes wondered why they didn't break up like an aircraft would if it hit the water at this speed. But it would surface a second later with a fish in its beak.

Chris and I went out snorkeling on the reef outside English Harbour one day. We were only out for an hour and a half but I saw almost as much in that hour as I had in the entire trip. We followed a school of brightly coloured fish around for a while; they gave way to smaller and even more brightly coloured ones. Then we saw some divers. It was obvious which one was the instructor and which the student. One was slow and comfortable while the other was flapping around and breathing much faster. She also had an air tank twice the size of his. Suddenly the instructor gave a throat slit/kill sign. It was fascinating to watch the student respond: she swam over, took her mask off and, together, they surfaced, breathing from a bubble of cupped air. I know this is in the basic training but to watch it from above, in practise, was a treat.

Just as they surfaced a turtle swam by. We followed it for ten minutes. It didn't seem to be at all worried by us. He just wandered around a bit like us, almost as if he was snorkeling too. At times he would drop down to the sea bed six metres below us, while at others he would swim a metre below us. I could have reached out and touched him. Finally, after we had drifted a long way with him, we decided to return, across the harbour entrance, back to our dinghy. Suddenly, right in front of us, just below the surface, a barracuda swam by. I had only seen them on the end of my fishing line or in a fishmongers before. Here, I could see what a killing machine they are. He was in slow forward mode, scanning the sea around him. He looked like he could accelerate fast. His jaw was lined with the same lines of sharp teeth as when Kelly and I tried to free Barry but this one's were ready to pierce. Any small fish in the vicinity was at risk. In the space of two minutes we had seen one of the most docile creatures and one of the meanest. We were both a bit high when we got back into the dinghy.

Every week day morning at nine o'clock the English Harbour radio broadcasts the weather, and anything of note, in an incredibly English, female voice. She also makes some announcements. Less than a week before the start of Classics week she announced that the race committee were looking for someone to help out with results. The person needed to have working knowledge of databases, spreadsheets, web communications, yacht racing and handicap scoring. I had been planning to blag a place on one of the classic yachts but this seemed to be made for me. I had an informal interview with the Chair of the race committee and was soon brushing up on all my scoring knowledge. I then discovered that I would be on the Committee Boat, out on the water at the start and finish lines. Not only that but we were on a motor yacht with all food and drinks provided. And I would get a Classics Week, Mount Gay, red baseball cap. These are one of those items that achieve a value far higher than their worth. On eBay they are going for twenty five US dollars; no one takes them off because they might lose them. There are not enough for all the crews. I wondered if they deliberately increase the demand by reducing the supply as a marketing trick. I also got a committee polo shirt. I was a kid, happy as Larry, again.

It was great fun. Although the concentration on accuracy of starts and finishes was very tiring, my exhaustion came mainly from getting up at six o'clock every morning after nights of partying. There were issues with my phone, the web link, the database itself, the idiosyncrasies of the racing, plus my typos. Once I added an hour to the finishing time of one yacht. Luckily, there is a self correcting mechanism: a visit from the disgruntled skipper! All this meant that I rarely finished before seven in the evening, just in time to join the parties on the boats or in the clubhouse. I only got to eat properly one night that week. I made up for it by demolishing half the sandwiches on the committee boat.

It was great to be out on the water, watching the races. The sixty plus boats, ranging from twenty four to over a hundred feet, looked splendid as they sailed around. There were four starts for the different classes so they were spread out across the water. The courses are designed to make it easy to sail them and to keep close to the headlands for the spectators. It's all in the spirit of Classics Week.

Even so, there were some serious racing moments. Seeing the massive J class boats jockeying for position on the start line was breath taking. One of them, along with two other large yachts, was ganging up on the other. They kept turning across the line, stealing her wind, stopping her going to where she wanted to be on the line; as we counted down the start they all turned on to the line to accelerate; several hundred tons of yachts, within a few metres of each other, screamed across the line within seconds of the gun. And we were watching this from within hailing distance.

At the other end of the scale Rosa, with a crew of more than twenty, took advantage of a lull in the wind to go swimming. One of the safety boats screamed over to them thinking that they had fallen overboard. But no, they were playing. On the

Sunday, after the race, the boats all parade around English harbour. Rosa did it all by sail. With her tan sails, her jib and staysail out from the bowsprit and her wide stern she was an enchanting sight. I was really glad that the Spirit of Classics Prize went to "the always sailing, always smiling" Rosa.

During the week I finally "got" Antigua: it's a cuckoo's nest. We were essentially a bunch of European tourists, on an extended nautical holiday. None of us belonged there; we all arrived and stayed, some longer than others. The Antigua Race Week would be the unofficial end to the season. All the cruisers, charter yachts and racing yachts would move on. Within weeks it would be quiet again; anyone sailing in here would find the harbours empty, the party over.

I've noticed during this trip, that my mind starts to prepare for the next stage while I'm still finishing the current one. My mindset was turning to the Easterly crossing to the Azores and home. But there was something still nagging me. I realised that while I'd been over here my notes read like a series of postcards, a collection of travelling anecdotes. After the crossing I had moved from a traveller to a tourist. I had scratched a little at the surface in Bequia and St Lucia but looking back I realised I have been disappointed in the Eastern Caribbean. I didn't like being seen as a source of income. The places I have enjoyed most have been where the yotties are insignificant in the lives of most inhabitants. Over here the businesses have turned to face us. But it wasn't just that. I felt a general lack of creativity. I'd seen very few live bands and most of them had covered UK or USA songs. Almost all the reggae was Bob Marley, who'd died over twenty years ago. There seemed to be a lack of spark, a lack of ambition. I say this carefully; I'd met people doing some very impressive things. It was just a general, underlying feeling I'd got. Until the crossing I had been concerned with the challenge of getting here. Once here I had not had, apart from thinking about the return crossing, too many challenges and, apart from some occasional exchanges, I had not really explored any cultures. Perhaps I was partying too much to make an effort to understand how the countries ticked.

I'd received a couple of emails, from the UK, telling me how the combination of an unseasonably hot spring with the convergence of a late Easter, a May bank holiday and a royal wedding had effectively closed the UK for two weeks. I was obviously concerned about the return trip as I became jumpy, occasionally tense. I started preparing the boat. The fuel dock was a dinghy ride away across English Harbour; a few trips back and forth and I had both the water and fuel tanks full plus extra in jerry cans. I wanted to get food sorted too but the supermarket was two bus rides away and they wouldn't take kindly to me carrying loads of bags on the bus. I had to wait until I could get around to Jolly Harbour where I was going to check out of Antigua. I kept wondering how I had managed twenty four days on my own coming over. Was I really going to do it again? The winds were not going to be so predictable and I may get caught in gales or calms; or both.

A weather window opened up. Unfortunately, it was the day after a Public Holiday so I couldn't get my gas bottles filled or my washing done in time. I spent all my spare time working out how I could get everything fitted in to the Tuesday and go. But then the wind got up further. All the adrenaline of preparation was wasted. I slept until half past two. I went over to see the Rosa crowd, hoping that I could relax and enjoy their company. It worked to some extent but I was still like a character in a Tennessee Williams play. They were relaxed though; they had sorted out delivery jobs for those staying and had plans for those sailing back to Falmouth. While I was there a phone call came through to one of Rosa's crew: "Anyone want a job on a motor launch back to UK? Start tomorrow. $150 US per day." I did consider it. I would get a flight back to Antigua in the deal, the best part of a $1000 and it would be a relaxing, almost boring journey. But I decided it would spoil the essence of this year to get back to the UK without Safe Arrival.

The delay meant I was still in Antigua for Race Week. This has none of the fun atmosphere of Classics Week. It's full of charter holiday crowds coming out for a week of racing. They don't socialise between boats and there's no camaraderie amongst the crews. But they did have an aquatic form of "It's a Knockout" competition during the lay day. They had teams trying to knock each other off a float using only a metre long inflatable hand. There was a greasy pole (a wooden mast laid horizontal) and a tug of war between Optimist dinghies. The whole team was in the dinghy so the freeboard was less than 10 cms. Great cheers went up as a team paddled too hard and their boat sank.

Spike, from Rosa, had been approached by a rum company marketing team for the use of his tender, Ellie May, a clinker sailing boat. They wanted him to scull a Captain Jack Sparrow lookalike around while he advertised the rum. It was a wonderful sight: Spike had obviously no time for this person in his boat. He sculled with all the contempt he couldn't hide while he not once looked at him. It turned out that the actor had managed to offend Spike and rubbish his lifestyle/boat in the first minute of their meeting. As the actor got out his microphone the comedy improved: his accent was worse than Johnny Deppe. It ranged through English, Irish and Scottish in the space of one sentence. And he appeared to be getting seasick in a dinghy.

At last the weather looked good. I spent the last night quietly and, in the morning, gently pulled my anchor up. It had been lying in the gloopy mud for several weeks. There was all sorts of vegetation attached to the chain along with what mud hadn't stayed on the bottom. It stank. As I left the harbour I dropped the bucket while trying to wash the gloop off the deck.

I sailed around to Jolly Harbour where I had a good big lunch, cleared customs and immigration and provisioned up. I met Barry and Ann for a quiet evening drink, a burger and a shower before leaving them my last Eastern Caribbean dollars - I wouldn't need them again - and rowed quietly back to the boat.

14 EAST CROSSING

In the morning Barry and Ann came by for a last cup of tea and to help me stow the outboard and the dinghy. Then they went to watch the Manchester City match while I quietly dropped the mooring buoy and left. I was off.

For the first two days I made good progress; more than 100 miles per day. I avoided Barbuda, a long island reef and beach, hardly any height above the sea, and tried to head North with a bit of East. Unfortunately, despite the good winds, I managed to head a bit West away from the Azores. Up until Grenada the compass had always pointed South and/or West. From then on it has pointed North and/or East. Now here I was, making West again. On the third day the wind died for several hours before coming back from the North. I could head North East. Although this was towards the Azores it would also take me towards the Sargasso Sea, that becalmed, current-less sea in the middle of the North Atlantic. Over the next few days I was in very light winds or no winds at all. At one point the water was so glassy that I could see way down into it. Intrigued I wondered how far down. I got out the plumb line to see. I lowered the weight down: it was over ten metres before I lost sight of it.

It was very hot. The decks burnt my feet. I had a headache. I splashed water over the decks to cool them but they soon heated up again. I poured buckets of water over my head to cool down. Down below was like an oven. I tried using a plant spray to make a mist and then walk into it but, within minutes, the temperature had soared again.

I noticed three little fish hiding in the shade under the boat. The bigger one looked large enough to eat so I got out my line and lure to tempt it. At first they sniffed it and went away but I noticed that if I threw the lure past them and pulled by they would sniff it again. So then I pulled it fast and out of the water.

I was properly fishing for the first time in my life. And, in a couple of minutes, I caught one. I had seen the type in the aquarium in Guadeloupe. I couldn't remember its name but I called it a Disney fish. Dark blue with a flat but oval shaped body it had long eyelashes. I ate it for lunch.

In this flat calm I was just short of catching the coat tails of a depression about 100 miles north of me. I motored for a little while to see if I could get to it but without success. Over a few days my daily run reduced to about 40 miles a day. In my calculations I worked out that it would take me thirty five days to get to Horta; somehow that didn't seem to be a problem. Once at sea it is meaningless to try and measure a long passage in more than a few days. Each day is a different day to the next although they run into each other in my memory after a few more. Sometimes I couldn't remember if I'd had pasta or rice the day before or two days before that. After an audit of my food and water I realised that I could last for forty days so I wasn't worried about surviving. My main concern was that I'd told Rob not to worry unless I hadn't contacted him by 5th June. I had visions of a search party scanning the Atlantic for me. Then it occurred to me that I was occasionally within VHF range of tankers and cargo ships when they passed. I would call them for weather updates and, occasionally, to ask if they were aware of my presence; it would be easy to ask one of them to send an email for me or to report my position.

Slowly, I made a few more days north before I caught a new depression. At first it was just enough to fly the spinnaker for a few days but then it got stronger and I had to reef. Looking back I can see that I was much more relaxed about sailing now. I seemed to be so much in tune with the weather that I could tell that there would be no change. I'd left the spinnaker up for nearly three days. Just as I seemed to be set for a good run the clouds came in and I was windless again. I worked out that this must be an eddy from the main depression. By the time I got out of this one the main one had moved away. I was left with a massive high pressure system that covered most of the mid Atlantic. North of it the systems were battering the UK and Scandinavia; south of it the trade winds were still blowing towards Grenada. The sea temperature had cooled noticeably. Once again I came to terms with the prospect of a long passage. My estimates for the crossing had ranged from twenty five to thirty five days. Except for keeping count in the log book I really had no idea how long I had been going; the day had run into each other so much that counting them had become irrelevant. My world was punctuated by two events: the sun coming up and going down. In these light winds the sea was practically flat; there was no change in the colour of the waves from day to day; it was just light or dark. After some time a light wind came from the south east. I could now make a pleasant course for Horta. This wind kept with me for several days. It seemed to be caused by the slight cooling of the high pressure in the evening; this would diminish slightly during the day and return stronger at night. The sea was nearly flat as I made my way through this undying view.

A week or so later a passing tanker told me to expect gales nearer to the Azores. I didn't get a gale but the wind turned against me and I had to tack. After two days of tacking I had managed to journey eighty miles on, but Flores was still 130 miles off. The wind died mid-afternoon; it was not possible to shape a course for this most easterly and, reputedly, very pretty island. For four hours we were against the swell of the old gale to the east; the sails would repeatedly snap, lazily against the roll of the boat, as the swell passed under us. There were thick clouds at dawn, some low and grey. There was rain below them, hanging gloomily in the space above the sea. The grey sea reflected the clouds in the slow swell. Everything was held heavy by its own stillness. Occasional wisps of wind gave us a slow movement, an attempted dawdle in the lolloping sea. Even though it got brighter later the mood was not lifted; the sun was trying to break through the blanket clouds but this only seemed to highlight the, not quite, stillness.

Calculations entered my head: could I get close enough to motor? What day would I get to Flores at this speed? Why couldn't the wind have held for another three days? I'd be there by now. Was I going to spend the whole of May at sea? I'd been wearing my foulies often enough now for it not to feel unusual. When I had first put them on I had to free the zips of all the salt that had accumulated over the months of storage. I worked out that I hadn't worn them since the day I left Portugal. On this trip I was into a routine that I wore them at night but that, during the day I stripped to shorts and back again as the midday sun came and went. By afternoon we had brilliant sunshine again and a light north easterly wind gliding us across a now flat sea. I sat in the cockpit listening to an Ian Rankin story: The Naming of the Dead. Unfortunately, the last CD was missing so I never found out who done it, or even completely what they'd done.

As the sun set on the twenty seventh day I was close enough to motor. With the engine on I had enough power to keep the laptop on so I watched a movie. It felt very strange to be sitting in my saloon, earphones on, watching the Da Vinci Code. I slept well that night, only waking to check for other traffic, and rising with a glorious dawn. I was motor sailing faster than at any other time of the passage. Suddenly, right in front of me, Flores appeared. There was no gradual grey outline on the horizon; it just appeared about thirty miles away. I whooped and brayed and was very, very happy. I was going to make land before nightfall. I had lunch, prepared food for the rest of the day, put some water in the tank and had a shower. I could afford to be generous with water again as I now knew I could soon get some more.

Slowly, features appeared on the island landscape. After a few more hours I could see houses. I turned on the phone; a picture of the view from my Bristol bedroom appeared on the screen. Suddenly I had a stab of homesickness. There I was, about to make land in this furthest west part of the EU and I wanted to be home. I turned on the stereo and played some music, loud, danced and felt better.

I checked the chart for a safe approach, rounded the south end of the island and made for Lajes. A couple of hours before I reached it I heard a boat calling to anyone in the harbour. The pilot book is very out of date and they wanted to know what the form was. I took note of the name of the boat, Moody Fin, and called them when approaching. They told me that it was a tight, small marina with no staff, no electricity, no water and no charge. I rounded into the outer harbour, dropped sails, prepared lines and fenders and spotted the marina hiding in the corner between a large breakwater and several large rocks. There were only a few metres between them. Tight was an understatement. I have never seen pontoons so close to each other. Safe Arrival is a relatively small boat but I could only just go onto a finger pontoon. All the larger boats had devised interesting means to hold onto them. I turned in through the tiny gap in the breakwater, turned 180 degrees to see them waving me around the end of what could be defined as a gap but it looked like a hole between two boats. My pontoon involved me turning 270 degrees in very little more than my own boat length. This was the first time I had made a finger pontoon approach in more than 6000 miles and six months. Keeping the panic down I tried to remember all the things to do while I turned in front of five helpers. It was OK. They took the lines while John from Chalone, last seen in Antigua, said "Hi Matt, come for supper." That was a nice welcome.

That night we had a few beers up at Paula's. Paula is the local entrepreneur; she has fingers in loads of pies and speaks English with a Bronx accent. She runs the beach hut bar up the hill overlooking the harbour. Talk to her and she will organise or procure whatever you want. Hire car? No problem. Laundry? She will return it within eighteen hours. Diesel? Give her your jerry cans and her husband, who runs the local garage, will drop them off an hour later. For large amounts you could ask the bowser to come to the marina but this would involve the police, ambulance and fire service being in attendance so it doesn't often happen. Instead Mr Paula will arrive with hundreds of cans on the back of his pickup. For the rest of the day you can see the yotties sitting on the deck, siphoning diesel into their tanks.

On the way back we spotted three yachts coming in in the dark. One of them appeared to be hesitant. We hurried down to help them, John guiding them by radio. We were never sure, afterwards, what part of "leave the red light clear to port" they didn't understand but they drove straight into the breakwater on the wrong side of it. There was a horrible squeaking crash sound and the wife calling out on the radio. Moody Fin hurriedly got their dinghy down and started putting the outboard on it but the boat managed to get off the rocks. There was no room for them on the pontoons so we guided them on to the wall where we took their lines and made them secure. It was a forty five foot yacht with a husband and wife team. They'd set off from Bermuda, a twelve day sail, but managed to run out of water; two people with at least two water tanks of at least 200 litres each. Had they both had showers twice a day? We left them to get themselves sorted and I went to bed, happy that I was over the longest solo period of my life and that Safe Arrival had lived up to her name.

15 THE AZORES: THE FINAL CROSSROADS

Flores was a very clean island. The roads were all in good condition, the houses were all whitewashed or in modern render, the pavements were free from clutter and the air fresh. The strange thing was I couldn't see any people. There were the occasional gatherings of a few men in the widely dispersed bars but there seemed to be about three houses for every person visible. The streets were deserted. I walked for ages, trying to find a supermarket, and without finding anyone to ask the way. Every spare patch of earth was filled with vegetables. Potatoes were growing everywhere. The fields were lusciously green and... there were Jersey cows. It made me feel partly at home but also highlighted the long way I still had to go.

When I first arrived I thought that I had heard kids playing with kazoos. John and I were walking back down from the town when I heard these sounds in the darkness. They were similar to Punch when he hits Judy: "That's the way to do it!" but the words were indistinct. Maybe it was because they were in Portuguese. But, slowly, as I heard more of them across the island, it dawned on me that these weren't kids; they were birds. There are hundreds of these birds flying around sounding like Punch and exclaiming in loud terms to each other. In breaks between conversations we would all start laughing as we heard one of them 'say' something, almost as if they were joining in with us.

After a couple of days I felt I had exhausted what this most westerly part of the EU had to offer. The crew from Moody Fin had hired a car and took me around to the capital and over some of the hills. There was hardly any change wherever we went; it was all still, empty, clean and green. Santa Cruz used to be the port of call for cruising yachts in Flores but, since they built a breakwater, Lajes had taken over. We looked at the entrance to the Santa Cruz harbour and realised why; it made Salcombe or Scilly look like a walk in the park. Rocks all over the place, a couple of posts to line up as a transit and yet more rocks in the harbour. I would not have wanted to enter here after twenty eight days at sea. I was glad I had called in to this island but had no desire to stay.

I was now in a quandary. The weather looked superb for a week's travel north. With good winds I would be half way home in a five days. But I was not ready to go back to sea. I was tired, I hadn't provisioned, I wanted to see some of the other Azores islands and my brother was joining me for the last leg home. So I set sail for Horta on Faial. It was 135 miles away across a flat sea in light winds. With the motor on I was making good progress with an Atlantic swell behind me. By nightfall the wind had begun to get up. By morning it was on the nose and the waves were short and choppy; it felt like being in the English Channel and we were slow. There had been at least fifteen large ships around overnight and I had not slept much because I had had to stay to watch out for them. I was grumpy and tired. I just wanted to be there. Even when I sighted Faial it didn't seem to get any closer for hours. I went to the north of it to shelter from the waves and, eventually, rounded the headland into the sea between it and Pico, a classic volcano shaped island. The waves were now breaking in a strong breeze. I took down the sail and motored hard against the waves towards Horta. As I entered the harbour the breakwater did a brilliant job. I was in calm water and the weak sunshine was actually warm for the first time that day.

I had to raft up four deep at the reception pontoon. The last time I'd rafted I'd been in Brittany. As I arrived one of the guys who took my lines, Tor, invited me and several others to supper. What another nice welcome. But, before going, I went to look for a beer at Peter's Bar, a cruisers' institution. The service is not good there but it's one of those places where you walk in and you will be bound to meet someone else you had met on the circuit. Hails of welcome are common. As we entered someone called "Hi Matt." There were Misty and Richie from Rosa with Kate and George, two others from Antigua. They were on a delivery trip from Antigua to the Mediterranean. Of course we swopped crossing stories. After a good evening eating on Tor's boat I went to bed knowing that I was here for a while and could relax.

The days in Horta filled up quickly. When I'd arrived in Grenada I had months ahead of me with lots of exploring to do. I had moved on only because I wasn't sure how long it would take to reach Antigua or how long I would want to spend on other islands. In Horta my time was much more organised. I had to be back in England in time to go back to work. It wasn't so much a place to visit as a staging post, like Las Palmas. But, where Las Palmas had been the final frontier before leaving for the great Atlantic, Horta was a crossroads. There, boats were coming from anywhere: Brazil in the south to Maine in the north; and they were leaving to anywhere from Norway to Africa. It was truly international. One of the traditions, started in Horta, is to paint the ship's name on the harbour wall. There were hundreds, perhaps thousands, on just about every available space. They ranged from simple brush scribbling to carefully designed and painted (and some lacquered) logos. But for all these cruisers, most did not leave the bubble of the marina and surroundings. It was a case of stop, regroup, look around, and move on.

With John of Chalone, Dave of Red 5 and Carolyn, who Dave had met in Las Palmas, we formed a small community of single handers. We cooked and ate in an informal community rota. I hired a minibus to tour the island. Chris and Scot from Avocette had arrived a couple of days later so they joined us and so did Doreval and Katarina, a Brazilian couple who we had befriended in Flores. At the western end of the island the old lighthouse was ruined by a volcano in 1957. Rather than knock it over it buried the first two floors. So now the top half pokes out from the smooth volcano ash. It was originally smooth but Chris, who had been there before, said that the vegetation had taken over in the last few years. There was a mini-bulldozer removing this vegetation and smoothing it all back around the car park and visitor's centre. Presumably they were trying to retain the original effect of the eruption.

We moved on to the volcanic top of the island. We got the route slightly wrong so I ended up driving the minibus up a dirt track, hairpin bends and sliding dusty corners, right to the top. The people in the back were a bit quiet whenever they slid sideways on the corners. The crater was a lake for thousands of years but the 1957 volcano activity had opened a fissure so it was now a dry bowl. We walked around the eight kilometres ring, often on a ridge. We could see across the other islands and down to our boats on the marina. We were lucky; it is not often that the crater is not shrouded in clouds. We were in sunshine but across the sound Pico, the highest mountain in Portugal, was invisible. We could see up to a few hundred metres but the rest was in cloud. Jose, a Pican who we had met in Antigua, was going to show us around Pico but I had to leave before this was possible.

The night that Avocette had arrived we had gone to Peter's Bar again. Greg, an Australian, on his boat Rum Jungle, was rafted up to Avocette. He was very eloquent, well educated and combined this with a very earthy Australian attitude. He got quite cross with two of us single handers when we wouldn't big up our adventures. In his broad accent he said things like: "Now you guys have done this amazing thing and you could have the girls running to you but you hide it away behind your British stiff upper lip and I can't say it because I haven't done it. That makes me cross. Tonight I'm going to tell all the girls at the beach party about you and you'll see."

We did go to the beach party. We arrived about 2am to a small gathering of young people around a bar at the end of an isthmus. By 3am there were a lot more and Greg and Thor were chatting to any girls in sight. I stood watching, realising that, firstly I was about 25 years older than the median age and, secondly, I'd peaked far too early. Several beers and rums in Peter's Bar had fired me up for this but the interval between there and the beach had left me winding down. As Greg was "evicted" from one group of friends he was chatting up I went to say goodbye. I looked back to see him rejoining them, which he later admitted was a "tactical error." None of us were fit to climb Pico the next day.

With the minibus we made a supermarket and diesel run. Even with only five in it the bus was crowded when we had all bought our 'home leg' supplies. Bags were stuffed everywhere; and then we had to sort it all out when we got back to the boats. There was excitement and sadness in these preparations; we were getting ready for another passage but this was the home run. The party was nearly over for most of us. We compared notes on wind and weather forecasts, made our plans and then waited for the weather windows. Chelone and Red 5 left for Sao Jorge thirty minutes before I set off for Terceira the next day. My brother, Mark, was going to join me there for the leg to Scilly. This really was goodbye for most of the cruisers I knew. Having known them in various parts of a journey just short of 9000 miles around the Atlantic we would only meet after this as visitors. For most of us the cruisers' community would be a memory. On the other hand, we all now have ready-made holidays in all parts of the world; and, most definitely, there would be the next time.

16 TO SCILLY: THE LAST LONG PASSAGE

The last stage back to the UK was different. It felt like it should be quick, but the Azores are still a third of the way across the Ocean. I still had over 1000 miles to go. There was a way out. I could go back to Portugal or Baiona and take day hops. Then the only over night passages would then be Biscay and the Channel.

I was also starting tired. After twenty eight days crossing to Flores I had only stayed there two nights before moving on to Horta. That was an overnight passage and I had done another overnighter to Terceira. On both of these I had to stay awake because of the volume of shipping about. In Horta I had stayed a week but a lot of that was partying and touring the island. It occurred to me, though, that, if the passage was anything like the one from Antigua, I could relax and recuperate at sea.

I met my brother at the airport. It was good to see him after all these months. I'd already done all the shopping and topped up with fuel and water so all we had to do was spend the evening chatting over coffee and a couple of beers before we could set off the next morning. When he had helped me bring the newly acquired boat around to Bristol he had not shown any inspiring sailing skills. But when he had crossed to France with me at the beginning of this year he had been lively and dependable. He had volunteered to put a reef in, he had cooked and he had trimmed the sails. Because of this I had an expectation that he would be like this again.

Perhaps I had spent too much time on my own. Whatever the reason I found it a difficult passage. When at sea I do not drink caffeine or alcohol; both of these make me feel woozy. After a couple of days, once he'd settle in to life at sea and stopped feeling sick, he made me a drink. It was cool by the time I drank it and it was only when I'd got to the teabag that I realised that it was ordinary tea. It took me over a day to feel OK again after that burst of caffeine. It was little inconveniences of this sort, or my expectations of him being too high that made it difficult. If I had simply thought of the passage as me being on my own then it may have felt better.

For the first three days we had mainly light winds. We made eighty miles a day in slight seas. In this time it became clear that my brother had not prepared for the trip. However, we sorted out a division of workload and watches. We listened in to the shortwave radio each day. John, from Chelone, talked to us and Dave, from Red 5, three times a day. He would update us on the wind forecasts and anything else happening.

On the third day we were watching a large tanker a little way off when we heard it being called on the radio by Chelone. We looked south to see two sails a few miles off. I called Chelone up on the VHF but Red 5 replied. "Blimey, it's getting like Piccadilly Circus around here" he said. All three of us were within a small area in a very large ocean. We watched as Red 5 put up a cruising chute. The two of them slowly overtook us over the next few hours. In the dying wind all three of us motored over night. On our slightly diverging courses we watched them slip below the horizon as the wind picked up again and we headed towards Scilly.

That night we heard John telling us that a 'child' low system was going to pass north of us. We had seen the weather fax predicting that it was going to hit us so we were pleased by that. In the event, it passed right over us. All that day the wind built up from the south west. We were goosewinged on a run as we reefed more and more during the day and into the night. By nightfall we were fully reefed. In the night we took down the mainsail. I went up to the mast as we surfed down the front of six metre waves while my brother passed up the sail ties for me to catch and tame the powerful force.

As the winds increased further to gusts of forty three knots we wound in more genoa until we had a very little left. I suddenly thought to myself that we were in a Force 9 and that I was not scared and the boat was behaving beautifully. Here we were, surfing down these enormous waves, Mildred keeping us on course, the foam streaming off the top of every wave like scarves; and yet we could still make a hot drink safely. What a wonderful boat. I understood why the Rival 32 was praised so highly.

It was close to the end of my watch when I noticed the sky changing. It was a classic cold front passing. The visibility improved, the temperature dropped, the sky cleared to cumulus clouds and we could see the stars. I looked back to the compass to find that we had turned through sixty degrees. Mildred had followed the wind. All about the waves had stopped breaking but, still six metres high, they had become more like a swell. All around, there were lots of little mini-spumes of foam across the floor between them; little devils whizzing around like firecrackers in a crowd. In this relative calm I went below, off watch.

The next day was almost a mirror of the day before. Slowly the wind reduced and then died away. By nightfall we had tried flying the spinnaker but the wind died beyond even being able to fill it. It was difficult to believe that, in such a short time, we had gone from quiet to F9 and back again.

For the next seven days we headed north east on the south side of another depression. It was made out of two depressions merging together and appeared to be almost stationary. Actually it was moving at almost the same speed and direction as we were so we had a constant F6 or F7 with occasional gusts of F8. With this the seas built to a significantly high swell. The challenge was to reduce sail enough that the strains on the boat were not likely to cause damage but to have enough sail out to keep the speed up so that we were not overpowered by the waves.

During this time we related our daily position against our progress northward up the coast of Portugal and Biscay. Today we were level with Lisbon; today level with Porto etc. My navigator's madness returned but with a twist: my mental maths had calculated that an average of three knots would mean a journey of sixteen days, at four knots we would take twelve days. In light winds I would trim the sails to achieve that extra quarter knot. In these strong winds I, at first, calculated how the times that we travelled at five knots would make up for the times we were less than four knots. But now were travelling at six knots. The maths is easy: it was half the three knots time but my brain was having difficulty taking this in. Safe Arrival had never consistently gone that fast before. It was like living in a tube train. When down below the constant roar of the water rushing past the hull and the jolting as the waves changed was similar to travelling on the Northern Line past Mornington Crescent. This, and the constant vigilance for reefing, made this a very tiring passage.

Perhaps it was also that I was like a horse nearing its stable. Once we'd got north of La Coruna I felt I was on the home straight. I was beginning to enter familiar territory again. We might still be in the ocean but knowing that Europe and the UK were near made me impatient to be home. One day I turned on the radio to see if I could raise Radio 4 long wave for the shipping forecast. I was early; a few minutes before it was due. On came Test Match Special. There was something special about being able to hear the commentators discussing irrelevancies such as the distance of each test ground from the seaside and the delights of Mrs Smith from Chester's chocolate cake, interrupted only occasionally by the bowler's run up. And we were now on the Radio 4, shipping forecast map; we were in Fitzroy, heading towards Sole, Plymouth and Lundy.

On the morning of day ten, through the misty light I spotted Bishop Rock lighthouse. I had always seen it from the East before. It was one of my favourite views: from the Garrison on St Mary's, across St Agnes and the Western Rocks to Bishop Rock lighthouse and beyond into the Atlantic. Not only is it an impressive view, with the meanness of the razor sharp rocks forming crocodile tails into the sea, but it represents so much of our naval heritage. It is the end of the UK; "from Ushant to Scilly is 35 leagues." How did all those sailors feel, returning, without GPS, from the ocean? Now I had just an inkling of what it must have meant; it still sent the hairs on my back tingling.

By early afternoon we had passed south of the lighthouse, motored up through St Mary's sound and moored up in the Pool, an open bay that suffices for a harbour. With the dinghy inflated we motored to the little dinghy dock, made out of gigantic, buoyant pieces of plastic that fit together like Lego. Walking on these wobbly tiles, carrying the rubbish and water cans, made converting from sea legs to land legs interesting. I took my brother to the Garrison, past a football match in the world's smallest league of two teams, to see the view across the Western Rocks. It was still magnificent; but now it had even more meaning. I had arrived from the other side.

We had a meal in the pub that evening and made an early night. The next morning I ran my brother ashore for him to catch the freight boat to Penzance and home. By the time he picked up his key from my sister's house he had been away for twelve days, all of them travelling, with only two stationary overnight sleeps. She said he looked very tired.

17 HOME: COMPLETING THE LOOP

Scilly had the effect it normally does on me. I chilled out. Whether it was falling asleep by a lighthouse, or staring at the seascape, or drinking coffee at Juliet's Bar and Restaurant, the time drifted by. I must have been relaxing because I managed to get disoriented walking around St Mary's. I had navigated safely all around the North Atlantic and I got lost on a small island. I forgot all sorts of little things I meant to do while the day just seemed to pass me by. On my way back to the boat I bumped into one of my work colleagues and his partner; they were on the last day of their holiday. We arranged to meet for a drink in The Mermaid later after I'd got scrubbed up and eaten my supper.

Chatting with them in a pub was another slow part of my return. Firstly, I'd heard the shipping forecast and the cricket commentary. Then I'd seen Bishop Rock Lighthouse. I was back in Scilly, a place I've sailed to several times. Now I was drinking with a colleague. This gentle reintroduction was to continue all the way back. I was enjoying the atmosphere as we supped our imperial pints. Suddenly, I jumped up and ran outside: a Belgian cruising couple who had been my neighbours in Horta had just wandered by the window. We greeted each other enthusiastically and, just as enthusiastically, they joined us for a drink. As the drink gave the evening a rosy glow and a fuzzy edge to it, I was a little aware that my colleague may be overwhelmed by our stories of the last crossing. They had had just as boisterous a passage as us and we had plenty of stories to share. It was OK though as he commented that it gave him a good sense of what it must be like to make these journeys and, also, it gave him a sense of the brotherhood of the sea.

Over the next days I fell asleep in several places around St Mary's and St Agnes. On the latter I never managed to get across the causeway. Every time I got near it I'd sit down on a nice bank and doze off again. There is a nice garden where they encourage you to sit and look at the view while making a donation in a charity honesty box. It was a lovely view but, once again, I closed my eyes and drifted off. However, I did manage to get to The Turk's Head. This is the most south westerly pub in the UK. It is run by a couple who used to run a small restaurant "Over the Moon" in Bristol where I had eaten occasionally. It was fun to spend the evening with the mix of locals, both from St Agnes and the other islands, a couple of sailors from the mainland and a few campers. I began to realise that I had spent so much time with Atlantic cruisers that I had ceased to think I had done anything unusual. It occurred to me that what is considered normal is very much dependent on who you are with. I knew of at least five other single handers crossing the ocean; these people didn't know anyone who'd crossed. I told one of the sailors about the cruising fraternity and the breakdown of any political, economic, national or religious barriers; how we looked out for each other and joined in with anything. He agreed with me wholeheartedly. Sometime the next day I got chatting with a sailing couple who were new to Scilly. They had taken the ferry across to St Agnes because they were concerned that it may be tricky to anchor here and they wanted to check it out first. As it was likely I would have left by the time they got there I asked this other sailor to help them. "They're in a HR 36" I said as a way of identifying them. "Huh, they must be loaded" was his disparaging response; another little reminder of life in the UK. "You so don't get it" I thought to myself.

More reminders of UK life appeared over the next few days. I had to time my departure for St Ives with the tide. I'd not dealt with tides for the last ten months. Somewhere north of Lands End my mobile phone picked up a signal. I was back on my home network. As the wind veered to the East of North instead of the predicted North Westerly the trip was choppy, wet and tiring. To make matters worse the bay at St Ives is open to the NE. So, having arrived at ten at night I caught the next tide to Padstow early in the morning after a very roly night at anchor. It was the same: wet and bouncy, but the gloom slowly lifted and I arrived in some sunshine. I was welcomed by the harbour master to take my lines; he remembered Safe Arrival from last July. Although in St Ives I had closed the loop, having stopped there on the way out, it was at Padstow that I really believed it. To be back in the harbour; to go into the Old Customs House pub and to walk up to the supermarket and shop in pounds; this was where my sense of returning came home. I went to bed at ten that night and woke up the next midday. The sun was out. I had a shave and proper shower, got myself sorted and had a sundowner beer with my neighbours. It felt like a proper summers evening.

I had another boisterous sail to Lundy where, again, I didn't go ashore. I got there mid-afternoon and slept again for three hours. I played Amy MacDonald and Brad Paisley loud. These were the albums that I had played on the crossing to Grenada. I kept thinking of that passage; it was the first time I had been on my own for more than a few days; it was hot, I would sit out at night in just a t-shirt, looking at the stars; it was new, all unknown. Now it was hard to believe in this cold, UK summer. My tan was fading. So was my belief in the memories of the year.

There were several yachts at anchor. We waved at each other but there was no socialising. It seemed to emphasise my mood. What would it be like going back? I had fantasies of reunions with women from my past. Over this year I had often thought about this last stretch home; it would be the only familiar part of the journey; every other part had been new to me. Now I was there it seemed that my return was the new event. There, waiting for the early morning tide, I was in change, between the year away and home; and home had become the unknown.

The wind had died by the time I set off from Lundy so I motored all the way to Cardiff. As we were near spring tides, when it turned in my favour, we rocketed along. I listened to the last episodes of Hornblower and some music while the sun shone and I felt almost hot again. The shores of the Bristol Channel slowly closed in on either side and I began to recognise landmarks. There were The Mumbles, Nash Head. There was Ilfracombe, Lynton, and Porlock Weir. Barry Island and the headland passed as I turned towards Cardiff. I went out of the channel to avoid a cargo ship coming out. There was one waiting to go in too. And then another came out. In between times I managed to call Cardiff Barrage and get into the lock. Once through, Cardiff Yacht Club has a pontoon for visitors. I found it and got into the tightest alongside berth I have ever attempted. If I had been better at estimating distance I wouldn't have done it. The space was about half a metre longer than my boat. I was so glad that I got into it without causing any damage. To be one stop from home and injure a boat would have ruined my return.

This yacht club is on the edge of the conservation area of Cardiff Bay. It meant that I was moored amongst the reeds with ducks quacking around and a family of swans looking regal. I cooked my supper and went up to the yacht club. I say cooked but really it was heating up. Before I left my girlfriend had given me a carrier bag full of upmarket ready-meals as a going away present. I had saved them for bad times when I just needed a hot meal quickly. As this had not arisen I decided that I would start using them up. So for the last few days I had been eating these and the tins left over from the Atlantic passages. Another friend had given me a present that looked suspiciously like a ready meal. When I opened it, in Cardiff, if turned out to be some St Lucian chocolate. It had crossed the Atlantic once before she gave it to me and then twice again with me. Stuffed with upmarket chilli I went up to the yacht club only to find they do very good and cheap meals.

While I had been away one of my sailing friends had bought a catamaran which he was keeping in Cardiff. I could see one from the clubhouse. I phoned him to find out it was his. It wasn't, but the call inspired him to come over with his family the next day to see me. I was already meeting two friends (Bridge and Michala who had stayed with me in Lanzarote.) They were joining me on the last stage back to Bristol, so we made a party together, having lunch in the other Cardiff Yacht Club. We looked over their catamaran, envied the space and discussed the relative virtues of mono and multi-hulls.

We took the second lock out after low tide. The drop out of the bay into the vast acres of mud that is the Bristol Channel at low spring tide is quite dramatic. The bay is full of water and surrounded by buildings. The channel appears, beyond the opening lock gates, a land of mud, with fast streams running through it. With the speed of the rising tide it turned to fast moving water; we could regularly be heading in one direction but travelling thirty degrees off in another direction. The navigation is quite tricky so I was surprised to see other yachts heading out of the dredged channel. Did they know something I didn't? But then they rocked to a halt as they ploughed into one of the mud banks. With Bridge at the helm and Michala as lookout we motored past Flatholm where the council had recently opened a bar. We didn't have time to stop for a drink though. Further on, when we had entered the Severn Channel I called up Bristol VTS. "This is Safe Arrival approaching Welsh Hook en route to Bristol from the Caribbean" I called. Very nicely, but without any reference to last July, he gave me the information about the ship movements. It was obviously not the same watch as had called us up on the way out. However, there was a call back to them, from another ship, asking for our name.

It was the Matthew, the replica of John Cabot's boat that first sailed to Newfoundland. It lives in Bristol but had been cruising the South coast, France and Scilly for the last few months. The skipper was interested in my trip and invited me aboard sometime when we were back in harbour.

With only one minor error we negotiated the entrance into the River Avon. It lies between two large docks: Royal Portbury and Avonmouth. It is difficult to identify in that most of it is a mud bank with a narrow channel up close to the docks wall on one side. As the tide was running at about five knots we had to get it right first time. Otherwise we would be fighting the tide at full speed to get back to it. I was beginning to get excited now. The Avon is beautiful to sail up and it was sunny. I could see all the new landmarks as we rounded each turn in the river. Bristol Docks called us. They asked us to hurry or we would miss the stop gates. These are the inner lock gates that are closed on spring tides to stop the river flooding the docks. We hurried under the Clifton Suspension Bridge and on into the lock. I started to slow as we approached but they called us on. It hadn't occurred to me that the lock is so large that I could slow once I was in it. In fact I could have done a figure of eight in it with no problem.

We stopped. There were two more friends there to greet us. They came aboard as the lock keeper pressed the button to close the outer gates. Nothing happened. He tried again but still nothing. So we missed the stop gates anyway. A few minutes later they worked and we made our way through the gap of the swung bridge and moored up against the basin wall. I cracked open Azorian beers for us all. I climbed ashore with a beer in my hand and laughed; then nearly cried. I was home. I was back. Was it real? Had I dreamt it? Did I want to be home? Was I glad to be back? I felt emotionally mixed, confused, drained. I'd done it; but the year was over. I was back. It was sinking in. It had really happened.

Once opened, we passed through the Junction Lock and into the harbour; we pulled into Bristol Marina at about 10pm on Saturday 2nd July, almost exactly eleven months, forty eight weeks, since we'd left. I put the Safe Arrival to bed and we went for another drink.

EPILOGUE

I have absolutely no idea what day it is. I have been at sea for so long. Every day is the same as the one before, and the one before that; more than tomorrow is just too hard to imagine, anything before yesterday is just a thought, it is just seems meaningless. The wind is blowing, warm, from behind, as it has been, forever, since I left. It blows the waves behind me too. Each one drifts up, a valley approaching, from behind to form a hill of water. Each one passes under the hull; a little surge with the surf and we drop back into the valley. The sun has come up, and it has gone down. Nothing else has changed. I am on my own, in my own world, thirty two feet by ten, surrounded by sea and sky, alone in the darkness. Maybe, the closest people to me are in the Space Lab up there somewhere.

I am lying propped up in the cockpit, lulled by the waves. In the clear sky I can see thousands of stars, so clear, so many unknown stars. On the right, low on the horizon, is the Pole Star. It is small, it is significant only as a marker, to keep it on the beam, to keep me travelling west. The Plough has not risen yet, something I am still surprised by. There is another constellation that looks a bit like a question mark. It goes around the Pole Star like a twenty four hour clock hand, but backwards. If I applied myself I could work out the time. But as I do so I lose myself in other thoughts. Ahead on the left is Orion, imperious with his shining belt. Somewhere, low on the left, the Southern Cross will rise towards morning. The only colour in this enormous sky is the reflection from the mast light. At the top of the stays I can see a glimmer of red and green.

The wind is from the Sahara, more than a thousand miles behind me. My t-shirt is tatty, UV-faded and salty; about the only clothing I wear, a habit left over from my life, on land. My thoughts, wander in and out, leaving little trace. They seem to travel with the wind. I am lost, wandering with them. I am at peace.

It never leaves me. In the gaps between thoughts; when I put the lemon in my tea, or the marmalade on my toast; when I see a red light in the dark, or a map of somewhere I've been; a smell of sea air; the wind in the roof, a snatch of Amy McDonald - I am back, instantly, to those days, endless and yet over. Part of me will always be there, at sea, alone, warm and unworried, under those stars, amongst those waves.

I roll over, take a sip of water and look at my watch, the same one that hung above the chart desk for all those miles. It's 4.30am. I wonder what time would it be in all the places I've been. What would I be doing if I were there now? As I try to list them in my head they start to merge together. I am drifting off again, a boat in the current. A last question hangs though, like a dream, somewhere on the edge of sleep: next time?

GLOSSARY

Boom:	the spar at the bottom of the mainsail
Clevis pin:	a securing pin – like a split pin only stronger
Close-haul:	sailing as near to upwind as possible. Often an uncomfortable ride
Gelcoat:	the protective coating on the hull of some yachts
Genoa:	a big foresail
Goose-wing	with the wind behind having the jib and the mainsail on opposite sides
Gybe:	when the wind gets around the back of the sail and it comes all the way from one side to the other. It's ok if controlled but an accidental one can damage anything in its way, including heads!
Jib:	small foresail
Knot:	one nautical mile per hour; about 2 kph
Mizzen:	on some yachts there is a second (mizzen) mast at the back with a mizzen sail
Reef:	to reduce the area of sail so that the boat is not overpowered. Like turning down the burner under a kettle so that it simmers rather than boils.
Spinnaker:	the big, colourful, balloon sail flown at the front . aka: kite – similar to a cruising chute
Tack:	turning from the wind facing one side of the sail to the other side – because yachts can only sail about 45 degrees into the wind

Printed in Great Britain
by Amazon